Christmas
Miracles

Inspirational True Stories
of Holiday Magic

Brad Steiger &
Sherry Hansen Steiger

adamsmedia
Avon, Massachusetts

Published by
Adams Media, an F+W Publications Company
57 Littlefield Street, Avon, MA 02322 U.S.A.
www.adamsmedia.com

ISBN-10: 1-60550-017-8
ISBN-13: 978-1-60550-017-1

Printed in the United States of America.
J I H G F E D C B A

Library of Congress Cataloging-in-Publication Data
Steiger, Brad.
Christmas miracles / Brad Steiger & Sherry Hansen Steiger.
p.   cm.
ISBN-10: 1-60550-017-8
ISBN-13: 978-1-60550-017-1
I. Miracles. 2. Christmas--Miscellanea.
I. Steiger, Sherry Hansen. II. Title.
BT97.3 .S74   2001
242'.335--dc21   2001033550

Interior photo © Falk Kienas / istockphoto.com

Previously published as *Christmas Miracles*, by Brad Steiger and Sherry Hansen
Steiger, copyright © 2001 by Brad Steiger and Sherry Hansen Steiger,
ISBN-10: 1-58062-552-5, ISBN-13: 978-1-58062-552-4.

This book is available at quantity discounts for bulk purchases.
For information, please call 1-800-289-0963.

Dedication

This book is for our parents, children, and grandchildren, with whom we have shared many Christmas miracles in the past and with whom we hope to share many more such miracles in the future.

Introduction

The story of the first Christmas, as it is told in the Gospels of Matthew and Luke, is made up of the accounts of five miracles:

1. The Angel Gabriel appears to Mary, a young girl of Nazareth, and proclaims that she has been chosen for a very special purpose. God's holy spirit will visit her, and she, without knowing a man, will become pregnant.

2. An angel manifests to Joseph, a Nazarene carpenter who is Mary's fiancé, and counsels him not to put aside the young woman, who is now very much with child, or subject her to public disgrace, but to marry her. All of this, he is told, is part of a much larger divine plan.

3. Shepherds outside of Bethlehem, keeping watch over their flocks by night, witness a chorus of angels declaring the supernatural birth of a child in a stable who, according to the joyous heavenly host, will bring peace on Earth and good will toward men.

4. A miraculous star moves in the sky to guide three wise philosopher-kings from faraway Eastern nations to worship Jesus, "the newborn king," and to bring him gifts of gold, frankincense, and myrrh.

5. An angel appears in a dream to the three wise men, advising them not to return to the duplicitous King Herod with the identity of the child that he fears will usurp his throne. The angel also manifests in another night vision to warn Joseph to flee with Mary and the child to safety in Egypt in order to avoid Herod's jealous wrath.

Since the story of Christmas is founded on the five miracles listed above, there can be little wonder that miracles of faith and love continue to occur during a holiday season that has been held sacred for 2,000 years. For those men and women who believe that Jesus was far more than an extraordinary prophet and teacher, the true meaning of Christmas far transcends the exchange

of gifts, the gathering of families around the plum pud-
dings, or the decking of halls with boughs of holly.

Although there is the general belief that Jesus was
born at the hour of midnight on Christmas Eve, even
the most devout cannot attest to the exact historical
date of his birth. Even today, some branches of Chris-
tendom observe the holy birth in December, others in
January, April, or May.

It seems very likely that December 25 was selected
as the festival day because it also marked the advent
of the great winter celebrations of the Britons, the
Germans, and the Gauls. These days of merry-making
signaled the winter solstice and a time of great feasts to
honor the pagan gods. Although the early teachers of
Christianity prohibited any recognition of the ancient
deities or any aspect of their festivals as incompatible
with the heavenly character of Jesus, numerous customs
still observed today, such as the yule log, the holly, and
the mistletoe, reach far back into a pagan past.

By the fifth century, the observance of the birthday
of Jesus Christ on December 25 had spread to various
parts of the Christian world, and by the early Middle
Ages, Christmas had become the greatest and most
popular of all holidays celebrated throughout Europe.
By that time, churches observed the custom of col-
orfully decorating their usually austere interiors, and
they permitted actors to present religious pageants

depicting the Nativity. People sang carols in the streets, and there were numerous parades with marchers carrying aloft images of the Virgin Mary, the baby Jesus, Joseph, the shepherds, the wise men, and angels.

Since colonial times, Christmas in the United States has evolved into a period of great social activity. Because of its melting pot of cultures and customs, its unity in diversity, its blending of the contemporary and the traditional, America has fashioned a semisocial, semireligious celebration that enables everyone to wish everyone else a merry Christmas, regardless of an individual's religious expression. Christmas in the United States has become a colorful tapestry that has been woven together with the customs, beliefs, traditions, superstitions, and folklore of people who were once widely separated and culturally diverse and who are now next-door neighbors.

Washington Irving (1783–1859) wrote that during our nation's formative years Christmas ". . . awakened the strongest and most heartfelt of associations. There is a tone of solemn and sacred feeling that blends with our conviviality, and lifts the spirit to a state of hallowed and elevated enjoyment."

Christmas is a sacred time that touches many of us deep within our spirit—but it is also a time when we can put aside our solemnities and our stresses and become children again. We can stop being grown-ups and once again become the five-year-old boy or girl listening for the sound of Santa's sleigh on the rooftop.

And with so many hearts and spirits becoming open and childlike, what better time than Christmas for the manifestation of miracles?

In this book, we shall present a wide variety of miraculous occurrences that took place during the Christmas holiday. There are moving accounts of dramatic healings, inspirational stories of angelic interaction, life-altering visions, and joyous reports of the spirits of departed loved ones who briefly came home for the holidays. Christmas with all of its diverse attendant emotions truly does appear to have the power to open doorways between dimensions.

Each Christmas season, millions of men and women acknowledge the angelic promise of a peace that passes all understanding and allow themselves to perceive the world with childlike wonder and joy. Then, after the holiday has passed and they must move on with their worldly concerns, they too often permit the tensions and stresses of life to press in on them once again and squeeze the magic of the joyous holiday right out of them. And sadly, nearly all of the once hearty and cheerful expressions of peace, love, and goodwill to their fellow humans become absorbed in the day-to-day challenges of existence.

It is our earnest wish that this book might help all who read it to keep the miracles of Christmas alive in their hearts and spirits all year long.

SHERRY HANSEN STEIGER
BRAD STEIGER
Forest City, Iowa

Acknowledgements

There were many individuals who contributed their thoughts and experiences to the making of this book. Among those who must receive special thanks are Bob and Janice Kolb, Erskine and Charlotte Payton, Dr. Franklin Ruehl, Paul and Lorraine Lippold, Link and Hazel Olson, Bob Shortz, Clarisa Bernhardt, Cindy and Dave Bennett, and Dr. Bruce Goldberg.

*W*henever anyone asks Pastor A.T. Vermedahl about his favorite Christmas or a special Christmas happening, he always tells the same simple, direct, and miraculous story.

He was recently out of the seminary in Chicago 1959, and he found himself the shepherd of a poor congregation in a small Wyoming parish, whose elderly pastor had died of a sudden heart attack in October.

"I had arrived about a month before Christmas, just a kid in my mid-twenties, lonely for my family back in Milwaukee, homesick for a city with a main street that stretched out longer than four or five blocks," he recalled. "I really thought that I must be being punished by God for some sin beyond my awareness to have been sent out to this wide spot in a dusty road."

Pastor Vermedahl is embarrassed today by how spoiled and self-centered he was during his first days with the congregation.

"I am afraid that I must have appeared very condescending to the farmers and ranchers who sat quietly, reverently, humbly before me," he said. "But I guess they had decided to be patient with the smart-aleck city punk preacher."

With Christmas fast approaching, Pastor Vermedahl attempted to stir up enthusiasm among the choir director and the dozen or so members of the choir to attempt a seasonal oratorio such as Handel's *Messiah*.

"Or if that was beyond their range and reach—which, of course, I presumed it was—how about creating an original cantata?" I challenged the choir director, Mrs. Olive Martindale, the sixty-eight-year-old wife of a retired high school English teacher. "Or perhaps she could at the very least arrange a medley of religious and secular carols and hymns?"

Mrs. Martindale began to tremble and tears came to her eyes. He knew that he had intimidated her, but Pastor Vermedahl barely found it within his good graces to apologize and to tell her that whatever she came up with would be fine.

Two nights before Christmas Eve, it was Pastor Vermedahl who had tears in his eyes after listening to choir practice. But his tears were precipitated by frustration. The grand Christmas mass he had imagined was not about to happen here.

"Mrs. Martindale had done her best to arrange a bright and colorful medley of Christmas music," he recalled, "but there was so little talent among her vocalists that it seemed as though they were mourning the fall of western civilization, rather than celebrating the birth of a messiah."

Later that night in his study, Pastor Vermedahl telephoned his parents back in Milwaukee to wish them a merry Christmas.

"I was much more frank with my parents than I should have been," he said, "but, alas, I had the impatience and audacity of the young. Before I had graduated from the seminary, I had envisioned myself as the pastor of a large congregation in a major city, not as the caretaker of a struggling little community of ranchers and rustics. I found myself shouting into the mouthpiece of the telephone, 'I keep asking why I was sent to this godforsaken place!'"

The words were no sooner out of his mouth when he glanced up to see the shocked face of the church secretary, Mrs. Lankford, standing in the doorway of his study with the newly mimeographed copies of the church bulletin in her trembling hands.

"Pastor Vermedahl," her voice was barely a whisper, "we don't think God has forsaken us here in our little town. We very much feel that God is with us."

With those words, she hastily set the bulletins down on the table by his desk, reached for her coat from the rack, and walked briskly from his study.

Pastor Vermedahl said a quick good-bye to his parents, clicked down the receiver, and ran after Mrs. Lankford, trying his best to apologize, to explain that he was only using a figure of speech.

"And, of course, 'godforsaken' is a figure of speech," Pastor Vermedahl sighed at his recollection of the awkward moment. "It just happens to be a very derogatory figure of speech."

When he stepped up into the pulpit on Christmas Eve, Pastor Vermedahl felt extremely uncomfortable. He had no idea how many people Mrs. Lankford may have informed that their new, young pastor considered their little community to be godforsaken.

As if to compensate for his monumental thoughtlessness, he read with great enthusiasm the Bible passages from Luke that tell the ageless story of that first Christmas Eve, emphasizing with special feeling the verses that speak of the angels on high announcing the birth of Jesus to the lowly shepherds tending their flocks outside of Bethlehem.

"At that very moment," he recalled, "the door opened in the back and a beautiful young woman in a white gown walked down the aisle directly to the front of the church where the choir stood decked out in their red and green robes, waiting to sing their next selection.

"Although I had never seen the lovely woman with the reddish-blond hair before, I assumed that Mrs. Martindale had recruited a guest choir member. If this one could sing half as good as she looked, I thought to myself, she would vastly improve the quality of the choir. Since her snow-white gown appeared in sharp contrast to the other members' red and green robes, it was obvious that she was to be a special soloist on Christmas Eve.

"Without saying a word to Mrs. Martindale, who appeared rather astonished by her sudden appearance," Pastor Vermedahl continued, "the woman turned to face the congregation and began in a rich contralto voice to sing 'He Shall Feed His Flock Like a Shepherd' from Handel's oratorio, *Messiah*. Never had I heard it sung with such majesty, such richness, such command of phrasing, such appropriate emphasis. And she had no accompanying orchestra. The lovely woman standing before us in her almost dazzling white gown, singing a cappella, provided us with an interpretation of the work that was completely magical, enchanting, unworldly."

When she had completed the selection from Handel's masterpiece, the woman stepped down from the choir loft and walked back up the aisle.

"As every one of us in the church that Christmas Eve watched the beautiful stranger's graceful exit," Pastor Vermedahl said, "she walked back out the same door through which she had entered only ten or twelve minutes before. And she was gone.

"The four men who ushered that evening were standing at the two back doors—and they swore to a man that she simply disappeared into the cold December night. There were no vehicles of any kind in the parking lot that could have been hers. All trucks, jeeps, cars, and pickups were accounted for by the members of the congregation of the church still seated within."

Before the Christmas Eve service was completed that evening, the members of Pastor Vermedahl's little church congregation were whispering that they had been visited by an angel.

"And these many years later, I have no better explanation," he conceded. "I truly believe that we were visited by an angel of the Lord that Christmas Eve. No one in that region ever saw that beautiful woman in the white gown again—and they were certainly looking for her. Perhaps an angel was sent to us that Christmas Eve to demonstrate to everyone present—and maybe especially to a spoiled big city kid preacher—that there are no places in the universe that are 'godforsaken.' I happily continued to serve that congregation for another fifteen years."

*T*he year was 1955, and Bob Kolb, now a retired dentist from New Hampshire, remembered that it was his second consecutive Christmas away from home—and that particular Christmas Eve wasn't shaping up to be a very good one at all.

"I was sitting on a U.S. Navy ship, the USS *Piedmont AD17*. We were anchored in Subic Bay in the Philippine Islands," Bob recalled. "The temperature was in the nineties, and the ship was steel without air conditioning in the medical/dental sickbay where I worked. I was hot, despondent, and generally depressed. I just didn't want to be there."

The previous January 7, Bob had married his sweetheart, Jan, and on October 24, he had become the father of a beautiful baby girl whom he had never seen. He had no idea when he finally would lay eyes on her.

"I desperately wanted to see my wife, Jan," he said. "This was our first Christmas as a married couple, and here I was, many thousands of miles away from her, feeling worthless, defeated, and very sorry for myself."

Bob recalled that Jan was a marvelous correspondent. "She actually wrote a long and newsy letter to me every single day that I was away," he said. "And of course the letters since the baby's birth were filled with pictures and stories of this 'wonder child' that was ours. How I wanted to see my little daughter, June, and wrap my arms around her and my wife. But it was not to be this Christmas."

To make the men's pain of separation from their loved ones at Christmas even worse, a postal glitch had caused the USS *Piedmont*'s mail to be sent to its previous port. "So here I was in a distant land without one semblance of the things that I had previously associated with Christmas. There was no mail, no wife, no infant daughter—and a ship whose decks got so hot from the sun that even Santa's reindeer would burn their hooves if they attempted a landing.

The day their daughter was born, Bob Kolb's ship had been in the harbor of Keelung, Formosa, but he didn't receive word of her birth until a few days later. By the time that the wondrous telegram announcing her birth arrived from the Navy Department, the USS *Piedmont* was in the South China Sea heading towards Hong Kong to support the freedom efforts of the Nationalist Chinese government in their conflict with the Chinese Communist regime.

As they steamed along the coast of China, Bob recalled that they were often overflown by elements of the Chinese air force. Since one of the functions of their ship was ammunition supply, the crew often speculated on the crisis that would be caused if they were attacked by the planes overhead. An explosion of the munitions the ship carried would be horrible.

"But no attack occurred," he said, "and I arrived in Hong Kong harbor with one thought in mind—to get on the telephone and call Jan, who was staying with her parents in Philadelphia until I returned."

Bob explained that making an overseas telephone call in those days was so very different from today. It was not possible simply to dial a number. The call had to be arranged.

"The first step was to apply for liberty from my ship during the working hours of the telephone company," he said. "The second step was to go to the telephone company headquarters in downtown Hong Kong to plan the call. The call was segmented, and each leg had to be arranged individually. Initially, the call went to Tokyo, then connected to Wake or Midway Island, then to Honolulu, and finally to Seattle where it was tied into the continental United States system. Several hours later, the phone finally rang in Philadelphia, and I was talking to Jan."

Bob qualified that "talking" was hardly the correct term, because the quality of the transmission was so poor and the background noise level so high that normal conversation was impossible. The long-awaited telephone connection with his wife lasted for only a few minutes, and Bob was able to understand only two brief sentences: "*She has red hair . . . I love you.*"

"But it was Jan's voice that said those words," Bob remembered, "and I knew that she and my baby daughter were well. Such contact was so much more reassuring than a letter where you know they were well when the letter was sent—but you can only hope that everything is still fine by the time you read about it."

Bob said that the cost of that single phone call was $64 in Hong Kong dollars, and he still has the receipt to prove it.

After the USS *Piedmont* left Hong Kong, it headed for the Philippines where it was scheduled to do repairs and maintenance on some destroyers that awaited its support.

"It was early afternoon on Christmas Eve and my work in the medical/dental sickbay was over for the day," Bob said. "Because the Philippine temperatures in a steel ship became unbearable in the afternoon, we worked from 4:00 A.M. to 1:00 P.M., with an hour breakfast/lunch break from 8:00 to 9:00 A.M."

The men had several options as to how they might spend Christmas Eve. They could attend a movie that was being shown on board ship. They could read, write letters, or play the card game "acey-deucy"—the standard leisure-time activity aboard a U.S. Navy ship during that era.

"About a dozen of us from the medical, dental, and chaplain's department opted to have a little Christmas party," Bob said. "We all put our names on slips of paper, dumped them in a trash can, then drew names for the gift exchange at the party after evening chow."

The gift rules were simple, Bob explained: "The gift had to be something that you personally owned, and it had to have a monetary value not to exceed $3. Since we were all aboard ship with no stores or places to buy gifts—and since our personal belongings were so limited—it required a lot of ingenuity to come up with a present that might be of value to someone else, cost next to nothing, and yet be something that the giver would then have to be without for the rest of the duration. A real gift is one that actually diminishes what you have. A true gift is one whose loss will be felt by the giver."

That evening after chow, the men gathered in the dental department where there was also a small portable pump organ that Bob Kolb played at Sunday religious services when the USS *Piedmont* was at sea. Bob recalled that the chaplain opened their party with a short talk about home and what he considered to be the significance of Christmas. Later, while Bob played the organ, the men had some coffee and soft drinks and sang a few carols.

Then it was time to hand out the gifts.

"In order to prolong the event and the significance of the occasion, the gifts were given and opened one at a time," Bob said. "In addition, each recipient was 'roasted' a little bit to add to the fun. The gifts included such items as a can of shoe polish, a uniform belt buckle, a flashlight, a package of Navy stationery, a piece of fruit cake, a paperback book."

Bob received a toy roulette wheel: It was on a black marble base about four inches square that was painted red with black and white number slots on the wheel. In the center of the wheel, rising about three inches, was a T-shaped handle used for spinning the wheel.

The men said their thank-yous and went to bed. Work began the next morning at 4:00 A.M. Even though it was Christmas Day, the work aboard a ship must go on. And this was perhaps especially true for Bob Kolb and the men who worked in the medical/dental sickbay where there were always emergencies and people needing treatment.

As Christmas Day dawned, Bob remembered that he awoke with a new feeling of well-being. "It was as if all the depression, the heat, the frustration, and the loneliness were lifted," he said. "The feelings of desperation and despair were now replaced with a sense of accomplishment and camaraderie."

The loneliness for his wife and daughter were still there, but now Bob felt as though he were facing the sorrow of separation as part of a group of young men who served one another as members of a support team. The night before at the Christmas party, he had discovered that there were quite a few of the men who had children that they had never seen. They eventually loosely organized a group of the faraway fathers and called it the "Stork Club."

Bob's roulette wheel became a source of great fun. "I played with it for hours, using it to make charts on number probabilities," he said. "I also employed it as my personal 'guru' to answer questions and to create winner probabilities for our acey-deucy tournaments."

Bob recalled that the young dental technician who had given him the roulette wheel was Arthur Kitzman. "We were not close friends," Bob said, "but rather casual acquaintances. But his gift to me of that small roulette wheel was one of the finest gifts that I have ever received. In the nearly fifty years that have gone by since that Christmas time away from my family, I have been given many, many gifts. Many have been expensive and significant. Yet I do not really remember very many of those gifts. The roulette wheel, however, I remember in an intimate way—the moment of giving, the giver, the feeling of appreciation I experienced, even its physical feeling in my hands."

Bob Kolb began that Christmas Eve in 1955 thinking, "Why me, Lord?" Why had he been sent to a place far away from his wife and child? Why was this bad thing happening to him?

Yet, somehow, in a few short hours, his attitude had transformed him into an entirely different person. Now the meaning of "Why me, Lord?" was completely reversed: "Why have I been so blessed by you that I have been given all of this?"

Bob Kolb concluded his account of that Christmas Eve aboard the USS *Piedmont* in 1955 by affirming: "This, then, is the power of Christmas. A power that can in a miraculous way transform a young man from a state of abject depression and self-pity to a state of full acceptance and understanding. A power that can move a young man from the point where he says in anguish, 'Why me, Lord?' to a place where he looks at all the wonderful gifts and blessings that have been given to him and realizes that the wonder and beauty of Christmas is not in what you receive. Perhaps it is not even in what you give, but in God's love given in the form of an infant child, whose impact can perform a miracle.

"Night became day, apathy became excitement, and despair became a word that described my former emotional condition before the event that I now consider to have been my Christmas miracle."

*E*rskine Payton recalls Christmas 1992 as being extremely cold and snowy in Louisville, Kentucky—the coldest Christmas season that anyone could remember. Although he is now nationally known as the popular host of the syndicated radio program *Erskine Overnight*, during that particular holiday season Erskine and his wife, Charlotte, had jobs playing Santa and Mrs. Claus at the Louisville Zoo.

"By Christmas Eve, I was really tired of wearing the suit, the itchy beard, and hearing all the petty stuff that kids and adults wanted for Christmas," Erskine said. "I wanted nothing more than to go home, sit by a warm fire, and not even think of being Santa for at least nine months."

But Erskine and Charlotte had one more stop to make that night before they could relax. His beloved grandmother's birthday was on Christmas Day. She would turn 102.

"She had asked Charlotte and me to visit her on Christmas Eve at the retirement home—and she had requested that we arrive as Santa and Mrs. Claus to surprise her friends," Erskine said. "As weary as I was of being Santa Claus, there was no way that I could not do this simple thing to please my dear grandmother."

The roads were becoming slick but were still passable when Erskine and Charlotte left for the retirement home, loaded down with candy canes for the senior citizens.

"My grandmother's face really lit up when she saw us all dressed up as Santa and Mrs. Claus," Erskine recalled. "She wanted to show us off to everyone, and she asked that we visit with as many residents as possible. I did my usual grumbling protest, but with my two favorite women insisting that I be a jolly Santa, I had no choice but to utter my very best 'Ho, Ho, Ho's' and walk from room to room, itching beard, sweaty suit, and all."

After dispensing candy canes to dozens of the elderly residents and maintaining the persona of Jolly St. Nick for another couple of hours, Erskine was thankful that Christmas would soon be over. He was not yet at the "bah, humbug" stage, but he was getting there.

"I noticed a very elderly gentleman sitting at a table, head down, drooling, looking as though his mind was really some other place far away," Erskine said. "There was a young woman who I assumed to be his daughter sitting with him. In a kind of perfunctory manner, I put a candy cane in one of his trembling hands, not really paying much attention to see if he was even really aware of it."

But then Charlotte stepped forward and whispered conspiratorially to the old man: "You don't want an old candy cane from Santa. How about a little kiss from Mrs. Claus?"

She bent down and kissed the man's cheek, and he looked up at Charlotte and gave her a broad smile.

As the Paytons were about to move on to the next resident, they were somewhat startled to see the younger woman standing beside the elderly man suddenly break down in tears.

"She was sobbing uncontrollably," Erskine said. "I asked what was wrong and we tried to comfort her."

When the woman was able to regain her composure, she put her arms around Charlotte and Erskine and hugged them warmly.

"My father *smiled!*" she said. "He smiled when Mrs. Santa kissed his cheek. Dad has been here eight years and up to now he has never once changed his expression or given any sign that he is aware of anything going on around him. And now he's sitting there smiling, holding a candy cane! In all my life, I never received such a wonderful gift from Santa and Mrs. Claus as you gave me tonight."

Erskine saw that the woman was releasing blessed tears of joy. His beard stopped itching. The Santa suit no longer felt so hot and uncomfortable.

"I was now able to see the true magic of Christmas," he said. "I now understood that there is a Christmas spirit that transcends the rush to buy gifts, the rush to put up decorations, and the rush, rush, rush to spend extravagantly during the holiday. Christmas is a special time that transcends even the religious significance of this special day. That elderly man's smile was the best present imaginable for his daughter, my wife, and, yes, for Santa himself."

*J*anice Gray Kolb, author of such inspirational books as *Compassion for All Creatures,* said that residing in the woods of New Hampshire on the shore of a lake enables her each day to learn more about the wildlife that shares the beautiful environment with her and her husband Bob.

"Just a few days before Christmas 2000, I drew open the curtains on a sunny crisp morning to unwrap a stupendous surprise," she said. "There outside our sliding glass doors stood the gift of a huge moose!"

After exclamations of delight from her husband Bob and herself—and several moments spent in awe of the magnificent creature—Janice grabbed a camera and slipped quietly outdoors to begin a relationship with the moose that they would name Matilda.

The moose turned and ran into the woods when she saw Janice walk onto the front porch, but with

Janice calling gently—and Bob doing the same from the side living room window—the gentle creature gradually returned, stopping to munch on branches and shrubbery along the way. All the while, Janice was snapping wonderful close-ups of her as she walked up to linger along the side of their cottage.

"We watched her every move," Janice recalled, "and spoke to her in gentle tones, calling her Matilda. Rochester, our beloved marmalade-and-white cat, opted to observe the scene through the window from the sofa indoors. Bob and I gave up all we had planned to do that morning and spent two hours outdoors with Matilda. After all, how often does a moose come to call? Eventually, she roamed away from us, and we reluctantly went indoors. But the excitement of her visit lingered, and I wrote a poem to honor her."

Although Matilda did not return the next day, Janice had a vivid dream about her that night. "In the dream, she stared deeply into my eyes. I believed the dream was symbolic and required prayer and thought, but the initial interpretation that came forth was that she was a kind of spiritual visitation."

When the moose returned the second day, Janice could not help thinking of her as somehow "theirs."

"Matilda was so beautiful," Janice recalled, "and I was filled with awe at her size and gentle demeanor. I was so thankful that she was roaming our property."

The forest giant wandered into a deeper wooded area, and Janice followed. "She could barely be seen among the trees," Janice said. "If I had not known she was there, she would have been hidden. I moved in a bit closer, speaking gently to her. Still as statues, we both stood for an hour. Eventually, she became more comfortable with my presence, for she began to eat dead maple leaves and eventually whole branches. Another poem about her began to form, and I wrote it on some paper I had in my pocket."

And so it went during those days before Christmas 2000. "I passed many hours with this amazing moose," Janice said. "Sometimes I stood; sometimes I sat on the ground or on big fallen branches. But all the while I kept company with Matilda. When I talked to her, she would now turn her great head to look at me and make me feel acknowledged. Never once did she ever show aggression toward me. She could have walked or charged past me if she had so chosen, for I was no obstacle. Even when I occasionally took her picture, she seemed to ignore the flash. That she elected to stay made me feel honored, for I was in the company of a great, mysterious creature."

Though they had spent hours in one another's company, Janice will never forget that one particular moment when they seemed to blend awarenesses:

"Slowly she turned her massive head, and her big brown eyes stared deeply into mine from only ten feet away. I stood motionless, held by her gaze. Momentarily, I was in another realm. In my spirit I heard her say, '*I come peacefully so you may know me.*'

"My imagination? I really do not think so," Janice said. "As her eyes met mine, I was not thinking or creating, only allowing the contact. There was no fear, only peace. I could not move again until she shifted her head."

After the enchantment had been lifted, Janice took out her pen and paper to record the words left in her mind—while Matilda chewed on a green branch. Janice had always felt that the deer was her totem animal, and she had numerous pictures of deer in her writing room. Now a "family member," so to speak, had come, bringing with her a special spiritual vision.

Bob joined Janice near the lake, and they both took photographs of their mysterious visitor. Bob left as it was growing dark, encouraging Janice to accompany him back to the cottage.

"I stayed until dark," Janice remembered. "It was difficult to leave her, and I wanted to stay as long as I could in case this would be the last time that I would ever see her. I spoke loving messages to her and asked that she never leave our land or these woods near the lake."

On Sunday, Bob and Janice passed Matilda on the road as they drove up the hill to go to church. They stopped and backed up, and Janice rolled down her window and asked her to please wait until their return.

"On our arrival back at our cottage," Janice said, "we found her lying on our hill eating leaves and branches. We stood in silence as she rose to her enormous height, and we spent the rest of Sunday afternoon until sundown, observing all that we could about her."

Days passed and Bob and Janice continued to see Matilda, walking and talking with her in the woods or down by the beach as she stood next to their canoe. It was hunting season during these encounters, but Matilda was safe in their woods because they have declared them a sanctuary for animals with no hunting allowed.

"As Matilda continued to live in and roam our woods, we had a new spirit about us," Janice declared. "It was thrilling to share our lives with such a creature, and each day one or the other of us would stop for a moment and consider our blessing. Even unseen, her presence was with us, as we spoke of her and anticipated our next encounter."

Some years ago, Janice Gray Kolb discovered that in ancient Christian symbology, the deer is a symbol of Christ. "I have written about the deer being sacred to so many cultures in one of my recent books," she said. "Seeing those warning signs along New Hampshire's and Maine's highways about 'Moose Crossings' offers a signal both to pray and to think upon the marvelous creatures that roam these woods. Their very presence is transform-ing to us. Animals are messengers and they bring wis-dom to us if we are open. I believe animals can become spiritual messengers of mystery and transformation, and when we do not seek to learn from them, we deprive ourselves of their indispensable roles in our lives."

Continuing with this line of thought, Janice said: "As I live in the woods and learn more about wildlife, I am grateful for the privilege of witnessing each day filled with miracles. I believe that an enormous and precious messen-ger came to us in the form of Matilda—and that she is a spiritual presence that reminds us of our Creator. We had only to look into her eyes to realize the holiness within. I will never forget those moments when her eyes looked deeply into mine and touched my soul. She has forever left her mark—and should we never meet again, I am most thankful that she is out there somewhere, roaming our woods. And may she remain so forevermore."

Shortly after the series of encounters that Bob and Janice had experienced with Matilda, they read an article in a local newspaper about a moose sighting in another small town in New Hampshire. Accord-ing to the reporter, people left their homes and busi-nesses to view the moose. Motorists parked their cars and joined the crowd to watch the wondrous creature grazing atop a grassy hill.

"The article spoke of the mystical quality of the moose and how there was a quiet and awe that had come over the spectators," Janice said. "Even the reporter said that she had felt 'other-worldly' inside. She went on to compare the experience to the appearance of religious apparitions, such as when people report sightings of Mother Mary or Moses. For those men and women who believe, the reporter affirmed, Mary can be seen and Moses was an actual flesh-and-blood prophet who carried God's laws in his hands. And a moose standing in a foggy field for an entire day can be seen as a visit once again from God."

When Janice read those words in the local newspaper, all her feelings regarding Matilda were confirmed.

"When I was with her," she recalled, "it was as if there was a suspension of time. There was nothing else that I should be doing. God wanted me there with her. He had sent her as a gift to me—a part of himself."

As Christmas drew nearer, Bob and Janice used one of the many pictures that she had taken of Matilda on their Christmas cards, accompanied by the first of the three poems that she had written in her honor.

"To know that Matilda was right outside our cottage on Christmas Eve and Christmas Day, roaming our property and woods, brought a peace beyond all understanding," Janice said. "She truly was of God—a holy visitation to Bob and me."

*B*rad Steiger remembers a Christmas story from his childhood that his parents told him about a man's rebirth of spirit during the holidays.

As his parents recalled the story, it took place in the early 1940s during a lovely, but very cold, white Christmas in Iowa. A thirteen-year-old farmboy we'll call Marlin Sheldahl was very excited to be playing one of the three wise men who would bring gifts to the Baby Jesus during the Sunday school Christmas pageant. Every Sunday afternoon since the week before Thanksgiving, Marlin and two of his classmates, Gary and Roger, had been practicing singing "We Three Kings of Orient Are" and walking solemnly before the crèche that sheltered Elaine, who was portraying Mary, and Lowell, enacting the role of Joseph. A rubber doll wrapped in "swaddling clothes" had the important, but mute, role of the Baby Jesus.

For several nights before the pageant, Marlin was barely able to sleep. He went over and over his solo part in his mind, visualizing just the way he would approach the manger and kneel with his gift before the Christ Child.

But on the evening of the big performance, disaster struck the Sheldahl home. Marlin's four-year-old brother, Jake, started running a high fever, so his mother said that she was terribly sorry, but she would not be able to attend the Christmas pageant. She would have to stay home and look after little Jake.

Although Marlin was disappointed that she would not be seated in one of the front pews appreciating every note of his solo—and telling him afterward how good he sounded—Dad would be there.

As Dad went out to warm up the car, Mom put the finishing touches on his costume. Days before she had dyed an old towel purple, and now she wrapped it skillfully around his head and pinned one of her rhinestone brooches in the middle of his turban. She festooned his robe with braided curtain strings and bright ribbons. Marlin was certain he looked like a genuine ancient Asian potentate. The other kings of the Orient would probably be jealous of the authenticity of his costume.

Then Dad came in, rubbing his hands to warm them, and Marlin could tell by the expression on his face that something was wrong. "Car won't start," he said, shrugging his shoulders and emitting a deep, defeated sigh. "Battery's dead. It's this darn cold. Must be ten degrees below zero out there. Car won't even turn over. Sorry, Marlin. We won't be able to go to the pageant."

"Sorry" was simply not acceptable. He was one of the three wise men for Pete's sake! He had been practicing the song with Gary and Roger and his solo part for weeks. This wasn't Broadway. There were no understudies waiting to go on if for any reason he didn't show up. He *had* to be there at the Sunday school Christmas pageant!

His dad tried to reason with Marlin. There was nothing to be done about it. They lived two miles out in the country. It was bitter and freezing outside. What was Marlin going to do? Walk?

"I've got no choice," Marlin said, fighting back the tears. "I can't let the Sunday school teachers down. I can't let the other kids down. I can't disappoint the audience. What would they think if there were only two wise men up there? I'll walk to church."

"Come on, Marlin," his father protested, "you'll freeze! Probably get pneumonia."

"I'll have two kids with high fevers to sit up all night with," his mother added.

Marlin started to reach for his heavy woolen coat, then hesitated. If he struggled into his winter coat, he would mash his marvelous costume. He would just walk as fast as he could the two miles to town and the church.

"Wait," Dad sighed. "You're as stubborn as your Uncle Charlie. I'll put the charger on the battery and we'll have the car started in maybe forty-five minutes or so."

Marlin shook his head. He was supposed to be at the church in thirty minutes. The pageant would begin in fifty minutes.

"So?" Dad asked. "We'll get there just in time."

Marlin argued that that would be cutting it too close. He had walked to town lots of times. He knew he could be there in thirty minutes.

"You've walked to town in the summer, spring, and fall," Mom said. "Not when it is below freezing."

Marlin could not be dissuaded. He would start out walking. If Dad got the car started in a few minutes, he could pick him up. If the car didn't start for an hour, he would see him at the church and ride home with him.

And with that, the king from the Orient went out into the night, following the Christmas star that would lead him to the Sunday school pageant.

Marlin had barely walked down their lane when he realized how foolish it had been to leave behind his heavy woolen coat.

The air was so cold that it burned his lungs and stung his nostrils. Although his royal robes had seemed warm enough in the kitchen of their farmhouse, it seemed now as though he was practically naked. And the pointed-toe slippers his mother had made him really looked like something out the *Arabian Nights*, but on the snow-covered gravel road they provided little protection and warmth.

And now the viewpoint of our story shifts to the perspective of Emil Gunderson, the older gentleman who had the farm next to the Sheldahls'. Gunderson, in his late sixties, had a reputation among the children of the rural community for being a grouch who seemed perpetually angry at life in general and kids in particular. He was known to have a vocabulary of cuss and curse words that topped anyone's in the entire county, and the only time that anyone could remember seeing him smile was when he threatened to take a switch to some boys who tried to steal some apples from his orchard.

Emil Gunderson was listening to news on the radio when he happened to glance out of his living room's south window and saw something on the road that caused him to set down his beer bottle and focus his complete attention on whatever was slowly moving into the circle of illumination cast by his yard light. It appeared to be someone dressed in clothing of biblical times, complete with flowing robes, turban, and those strange pointy-toed slippers.

Emil hadn't been to church in fifteen years. He hadn't set one foot inside its doors since the double funeral of his wife and daughter. He had once been considered a very religious man, but God had betrayed his years of faithful attendance in church and nightly prayers by snuffing out his loved ones in an automobile accident. And his attitude toward Christmas was far beyond a simple "bah, humbug!" On his desk were three Christmas cards from his two sisters and one brother in Washington State. Those were the only cards that he had received, except for the obligatory ones mailed out by the bank, Bill's service station, and the Farmer's Co-op Elevator. He hadn't sent any cards in fifteen years.

He couldn't take his eyes off the strange figure walking on the road past his farmhouse. And as much as he tried to fight off the peculiar sensations that were provoking long-dormant memories, the robed entity seemed to be triggering emotions that he had long considered decayed and forgotten.

And then the robed being was coming toward his house. Emil felt his heart quicken. When he was a boy, he had heard his grandmother speak of having seen a robed figure enter a neighbor's house the very night that the man died. She had always believed that

she had witnessed the Angel of Death come to take
the old man home to the other side.

When he heard the feeble knocking, Emil hesitated for a few moments before he answered the door.
But he had never been afraid of man nor beast, so he
wasn't about to start now.

He swung open the door and was astonished to
recognize the older son of his neighbors.

"Mr. Gunderson, please," the boy was saying. "I'm
freezing to death. May I please come in? Just for a
little while?"

He stepped aside, asking the boy his name and
wanting to know why he was dressed up like some-
body from the Bible.

"I'm Marlin, Mr. Gunderson. And I'm one of the
kings of the Orient, you know, one of the wise men
who followed the star and brought gifts to the Baby
Jesus in his manger," the boy exclaimed, all in a rush.
"And I've got to get to the Sunday school pageant.
Our car wouldn't start, so I have to walk. I'm going
to be late."

Emil shook his head in silent appreciation of the
kid's spunk and determination. "You're half frozen to
death, boy."

Marlin nodded agreement. "Just please let me
warm up for a minute, then I've got to be getting
going. I'm going to be late."

"You're only halfway there, Marlin," Emil said. "You'll be a walking icicle if you try to walk there tonight in this below-zero cold. If it means that much to you, I'll take you there. Let me get the keys to my pickup."

At first the boy protested gamely, but he soon converted his objections to offering profuse thanks. Emil stopped by his bathroom to rinse with mouthwash to cover the beer breath.

Within a few minutes, he was dropping Marlin at the side door of the church where the young actors and singers of the evening's pageant were to enter.

"Won't you please come in and see our pageant, Mr. Gunderson?" the boy asked.

Emil grumbled something about having other plans, but almost as if another force was guiding him, he found himself parking in the church lot and finding a place in one of the back pews. He tried to ignore the heads that were turning to look at him, but when he glanced up from the program an usher had handed him, he saw that there were only warm smiles of welcome.

By the time that the Sunday school program had begun, several friends had stopped by his pew to wish him a Merry Christmas. And when Marlin and the two other boys stood up to sing "We Three Kings of Orient Are," it was as if he had been transported to another Christmas far back in time, when he was thirteen and he, Max Olson, and Dick Larson had impersonated the three wise men and had sung that very same song. In fact, he and Marlin had even had the same solo part and had probably even walked to the manger with the same old "incense burner" from the Sunday school prop department, the domed pot that symbolically held the frankincense brought by the travelers from afar.

With a soft chuckle prompted by his nostalgia, Emil recalled fondly how after each Sunday school pageant, the church deacons would hand out bags of hard candy and peanuts to each of the participants in the performance and to all the kids in the audience. How exciting it was to open those bags and look to see if yours contained a small toy, such as a tin whistle, a miniature Santa, or a decoration that you could put on your Christmas tree at home.

As he allowed the music and memories to carry him back to earlier, happier Christmas times, he saw himself no longer as a thirteen-year-old, but as a high school student, listening with open adoration as Rachel, the girl he would one day marry, sang a solo rendition of "Come, O Come Immanuel" for her part in the Sunday school pageant.

And then he moved ahead in time to another Christmas, when Rachel and he sat with pride as their daughter Connie stood before the altar with the other ten-year-olds and sang, "O Little Town of Bethlehem."

Soon tears were streaming down his cheeks, and since he hadn't brought a handkerchief, he had to get up and walk out of the church to get a tissue from the men's room in the basement. He had seen Marlin's father squeeze into a back pew just a few minutes before the three wise men sang, so he guessed he finally got the car started and Marlin would have a ride home.

Emil Gunderson sat in his pickup in the parking lot for several minutes before he turned the key, started the motor, and headed for home. He would call his sisters and his brothers in Washington state that next day and wish them a Merry Christmas. And he would discuss plans to visit them that spring before fieldwork started.

A thirteen-year-old boy in his Sunday school costume of kingly robes and turban, half-frozen in the December cold as he tried to walk to the church pageant, had rekindled the warm glow of Christmas in a heart that had forsaken the mystery of the season and exchanged it for the misery of a grief that had been nurtured for far too long. Just as the Christmas story tells of three wise men from afar who brought gifts to the newborn Prince of Peace, so did a little "wise man" prompt a gift of renewal to a reborn soul.

*E*unice York from Tulsa, Oklahoma, remembered that on her husband Sam's last birthday before he passed away, he had received two elaborately decorated cakes—one from his family, the other from a fraternal organization in which the Yorks were active. Even at sixty-two, Sam had retained a childlike enthusiasm for birthdays and holidays—especially Christmas and Halloween—and he had been moved to receive two birthday cakes, both delivered on September 29 to their door.

Eunice's birthday fell on December 26, and because she had come from a large family that had never had any extra cash for the observation of two special days in a row, she had been accustomed since childhood to having her birthday passed over without notice. Maybe a birthday card. Perhaps a present of stockings or a handkerchief. But never a decorated cake with candles and a personalized greeting written on the frosting.

Of course, the situation had changed after her marriage to the gregarious and fun-loving Sam, but on his last birthday she teased him about his having received two extravagantly large birthday cakes when she had gone so many years without having been given any cakes at all.

"Well, then, by golly, Miss Eunice," Sam laughed. "This year I'll see to it that you receive two big special cakes on your birthday, too."

Eunice appreciated his good-natured thought, but she only shook her head and replied: "Your head will be so full of Christmas, like it is every year, that you will forget all about my receiving even one cake."

Sam placed one hand on his chest and raised the other as if he were in court, taking an oath. "Cross my heart," he said with great solemnity. "You shall have two birthdays this year or my name isn't Samuel B. York."

Eunice would be eternally grateful that Sam had not sealed his vow by saying, "Cross my heart and hope to die," because her beloved husband died of a sudden heart attack one week later.

"It would have been unbearable to consider for even one fleeting moment that such a wish, regardless of how silly its intent, may have had anything to do with Sam's sudden death," Eunice said.

Sam York's unplanned and rapid departure from his well-ordered life would seem to have freed him from all earthly promises and commitments. However, according to Eunice, this was not at all the case.

On her birthday, over two months later, Eunice York sat alone, feeling sad and depressed. Their only son had been killed in Vietnam. None of her family lived near, and the people they knew in Tulsa were mostly Sam's friends and acquaintances and none of them knew it was her birthday. Of course there were a few close lady friends with whom she occasionally went shopping or played cards, but since her birthday fell the day after Christmas, she had chosen not to bother any of them about an additional celebration—and expense—during the holidays.

With Sam in his grave for nearly three months, there seemed nothing for her to do other than spend a night in solitary misery.

But amazingly, on that cold and icy night, a friend, Lorna, traveled across the city by bus to deliver a cake and a carton of ice cream to Eunice so they might celebrate her birthday.

"How . . . how did you know?" Eunice asked, unable to take her eyes from the sumptuous cake with candles, a floral design, and a personal greeting spelled out in frosting on its sides.

"I don't know if you'll believe this or not," Lorna began, a nervous smile on her lips. "I had just gotten home from work when it seemed as though I could hear Sam talking to me as if he were standing right there in the room with me. He told me that it was your birthday and that I should hurry out and buy you a cake with all the trimmings!"

Eunice was stunned by her friend's straightforward explanation of her birthday treat, but she didn't feel like interrogating her any further. After all, it was Christmas, a time of miracles. And if anyone could come back from the other side to see that she received a cake on her birthday, it would be her beloved husband.

Eunice and Lorna had no sooner finished a good-sized portion of cake and ice cream when Anita, the young woman who had been boarding with Eunice since Sam's death, entered the front door and walked back to the kitchen carrying a box that contained a beautifully decorated birthday cake.

Eunice shook her head in astonishment. "Anita, how did you know it was my birthday?"

Anita smiled and shrugged her shoulders. "I was just walking by the bakery, and I saw this magnificent birthday cake in the window . . . and I just felt like buying it for you. I didn't even know it was your birthday. I guess . . . I just thought I should buy it for you."

Eunice was certain that she had not mentioned the fact that it was her birthday to Anita, and the young boarder had never known Sam. "My husband kept his promise," Eunice York said. "Somehow, through the miracle of Christmas, he saw to it that I received two special cakes for my birthday."

*D*uring every Christmas season since he was a young adult, Bob Shortz of Dallas, Pennsylvania, has volunteered to work in some aspect of human services to provide for the needy and the homeless. For Shortz, the true meaning and magic of the holiday began on Christmas Eve 1958, when he was eight years old.

"My twin brother, Ned, and I were in the living room with our father, who was relaxing in his favorite easy chair after setting up the Christmas tree," Bob said. "It was our family custom to decorate the tree on Christmas Eve, and my brother and I were in a hurry to get started—but Dad said he wanted a chance to sit down and rest a bit."

The twin boys could not imagine how anyone would want to sit down and relax on such an exciting night. Grown-ups were so unfathomable!

As the boys paced the room, waiting for their mother and older sister, Wendy, to join them, Bob remembered that he began to quiz his father regarding a very important matter about which he had been quite concerned but had been afraid to confront. "Daddy," he asked, "how can Santa come down the chimney? Wouldn't he just end up in the coal bin?"

Bob knew that the chimney was connected to the furnace, because one of his chores around the house was to keep the "worm," a metal corkscrewlike device, covered with lumps of coal so it could draw fresh coal from the bin into the furnace.

His father acknowledged that that could be a problem for an ordinary person, but Santa was magic.

"You mean, the furnace can't burn him?" Bob persisted. "How does he get back out of the chimney?"

His father's voice rose just a bit impatiently. "I told you, Bob. Santa is magic. He can come down in the chimney just as far as he wants and then come out. Because of his magic powers, the chimney becomes an elevator. He can get out in the kitchen and eat the snack we'll leave for him. He can stop out in Wendy's room—or wherever he wants."

Bob seemed pleased that there was an explanation for what had seemed to him to be a troublesome aspect of the whole Santa-Claus-down-the-chimney scenario.

"By the way," his father said, "how about you two going up to Wendy's room to see if she needs any help wrapping presents. Your mother and I will call you when it's time to decorate the tree."

Bob recalled how he and Ned had raced upstairs to his sister's room. "Wendy had been wrapping presents from our parents to our aunt and uncle," he said. "She had already finished when we burst into her room to offer our services, so we sat on her bed and talked about what we hoped we would be getting for Christmas."

Wendy was a year older than the twins, so Bob knew that she was keener in the ways of grown-ups. He told her about their father saying that Santa Claus had magical powers that could transform the chimney into a kind of elevator—and he asked her if such a thing could be true.

"Hmmm," Wendy said, thoughtfully. "I've never seen Santa do it, but that must be how it works. Since he's magic, he can do anything, really."

Once again, Bob recalled, he felt reassured.

"We sat on the bed, looking out the window at the Christmas lights strung across the avenue," he said. "Suddenly Wendy said, 'Look! Look up at the moon!' "

There, in front of the moon, was a strangely formed cloud that projected a silhouette of Santa's sled so perfect and so clear that Wendy didn't have to explain.

"There it was," Bob said. "You could see the runners and the curvature of the front of the sleigh—and on the back was Santa's bag full of toys!"

Bob remembered how the three of them stared at the silhouette in thrilled astonishment. "You couldn't see the reindeer pulling the sleigh, but there was no mistake *who* it was that we were seeing!"

After the initial shock, the three of them raced down the stairs to tell their parents that they had seen Santa Claus's sleigh silhouetted against the moon, and they begged them to go to the windows to look up at the amazing sight.

"Mother hurriedly ran to a window to have a look, and Dad eventually left his chair to check out the hubbub," Bob said. "But you know how it is. By the time the grown-ups had arrived at a window, well, you know."

Their mother offered a sympathetic, "I think I see it."

"My, my," said Dad.

"It didn't matter," Bob Shortz said. "I knew what we had seen—and nothing could change the magic of Christmas and Santa Claus for me that year or ever since."

*F*ive months after the start of World War I, just after midnight on Christmas morning, the vast majority of German soldiers declared a Christmas truce in the hostilities between themselves and those of the Allied troops—the Russian, French, and British. Regimental bands began to play Christmas carols and the men raised their voices in joyous celebration of the Holy Night when the Prince of Peace was born.

The Allied soldiers were understandably suspicious about the shouts of "Merry Christmas" that they heard directed at them from the German trenches. Perhaps they had snipers lined up just waiting for a curious Tommy, Ivan, or Frenchy to peek his head above the trenches.

But at the end of each hymn or cheerful carol they heard the German boys from Kaiser Bill's army calling out something about a Christmas truce. The men in the Allied trenches checked with their officers, but none of them knew anything about a truce having been declared for the holidays.

At dawn's first light on Christmas morning, the German troops rose up out of their trenches, set down their weapons, and began to walk across "no-man's land," singing carols and shouting out, "Merry Christmas," in French, Russian, and English, as well as their native German. From all appearances, from everything the Allied officers could see through their field glasses and from what the soldiers were able to witness from their frontline observation posts, all the Germans appeared to be without rifles or any kind of weaponry whatsoever.

Soon the Allied soldiers crawled up out of their trenches and walked toward the Germans who were so openly and trustfully celebrating Christmas. The men shook hands, wished each other a blessed Christmas, and exchanged gifts of cigarettes and food. Later, they sang hymns and carols, and those of the same faith worshipped together. Some accounts of the Christmas truce even state that opposing sides played a good-natured, but rousing, game of soccer. The remarkable unofficial "time-out" that was declared by the combat soldiers without any thought of obtaining permission from their superiors lasted for two or three days.

Sadly, the Christmas truce of 1914 was probably one of the very last examples of old-fashioned chivalry in modern warfare. Within another few weeks, the first great technological war would begin slaughtering human beings on a scale previously undreamt of in any military officer's most fevered nightmare of destruction. The employment of poison gas against the men in the trenches, the aerial bombing of cities and civilians beyond the frontlines, the onslaught of armored tanks crushing men and smashing walls, machine guns mowing down ranks of soldiers, aircraft swooping down from the skies and strafing troops on the ground—all of these horrors and more would make the notion of another Christmas truce during the war an impossible dream. But the 1914 Christmas miracle created by the common foot soldiers' declaration of peace and goodwill toward their fellow comrades-in-arms will live forever in memory as a triumph of the indomitable human spirit over the fatal disease of war.

*D*uring the push to Berlin during the latter stages of World War II, Bryan Potter and a group of other bone-weary GIs were quartered in a brick farmhouse and told to get a good night's rest. The order was as unnecessary as telling a starving man to eat everything on his plate. The men were cold and exhausted in the bleak December of 1944, and although there was little to burn in the fireplace and the antiquated kitchen stove, any warmth at all was greatly appreciated.

They had just finished a sparse, but somehow comforting and filling meal, when one of the men started tapping his fork on his metal mess kit.

"Fellas," he said, when he had everyone's attention. "Do you know what today is?"

"Don't tell us it's your birthday, Skeeter," Potter said with a sigh of mock disappointment. "I am so sorry, I wasn't able to go shopping for a present. Every time I did try to go into town to buy something, those nasty Nazis started shooting at me."

"Can it, Potter," his buddy replied. "It's the eve of the birthday of someone a whole lot more important than this dogface GI."

And then the realization seemed to strike everyone in the crowded kitchen at the same time. It was Christmas Eve.

"For several moments, the room was silenced as we all became lost in our own thoughts of Christmas back home," Potter said.

"We were all somewhere else in time and space. Some of us were probably remembering a special Christmas Eve at home with Mom and Dad, sitting around the dining room table after a big meal, listening to Bing Crosby sing 'White Christmas' on the radio, all of the kids just waiting to tear into the presents under the tree. Or the last Christmas that we held our wives or sweethearts in our arms before we enlisted. We all wanted to be back home with our loved ones, not crowded into some German farmer's deserted home with the enemy all around us."

One of the men shifted uncomfortably on the hard wooden bench, then spoke up before he lost his nerve. "I think we should do something to observe Christmas Eve—you know, like singing a Christmas hymn.

Something like 'Silent Night' or 'Little Town of Beth-lehem.' "

"If he had been expecting ridicule from the hard-ened, tough men around him, he received none that cold and lonely Christmas Eve far away from our homes," Potter recalled. "Softly at first, as some of us struggled to remember the words, we began singing 'Silent Night.' Then as we got more into the spirit of the hymn, our voices became stronger and stronger until the rafters of that old farmhouse were reverberat-ing. By the time we got to the third verse, most of us were just humming along, but even that had a good Christmas sound to it."

Then, suddenly, someone carrying a bright light slammed open the kitchen door and shouted: "Every-one out! A mortar shell is about to hit!"

Potter and his buddies scrambled for the door, ran several yards, then threw themselves headlong on the frozen, snow-packed German terrain.

Seconds later, the demolished farmhouse erupted in a fiery explosion and began to rain pieces of brick down on them. Nazi mortar fire had scored a direct hit on their temporary sanctuary.

"It was a good thing for us that even though we were bone-tired, we simply reacted on our training and our war-honed instincts," Potter said. "None of us thought to stop to ask the stranger with the bright light just how he knew that a mortar shell was about to hit the specific target of our particular farmhouse.

"Whoever the guy was, he didn't burst in among us and shout, 'Heads up! The Jerries are going to start shelling!' He told us to get out because a round was about to hit us. That statement required special and specific knowledge, and if any of us had stopped to interrogate the fellow concerning the source of such intelligence, none of us would have survived the direct hit."

Potter and his buddies spent the rest of the night in the ruins of a barn, huddled around a sheltered fire. One of the men commented that Christmas Eve was the perfect night to sleep on a pile of straw near mangers and cattle pens.

"Later, when some of us had a chance to talk about the incident, a couple of the guys were already calling it a miracle," Potter said. "After discussing it at great length, we all agreed that the man who burst into the farmhouse was not carrying a bright light, he was the light.

"When we compared our collective memories, we concluded that the stranger was surrounded by a brilliant kind of illumination. We were convinced that an angel saved our lives on Christmas Eve in 1944 by warning us to get out of the farmhouse immediately before the mortar shell hit us."

When Don Checketts was a nineteen-year-old Marine stationed at Campo de Marte in Managua, Nicaragua, he became so homesick at Christmas for his family back in Ogden, Utah, that his wish to be able to be two places at once came true. A Christmas miracle enabled Checketts to visit his family in Utah and remain physically on duty at the Marine base at the same time.

According to Don H. Checketts's story in the May 1968 issue of *Fate* magazine, mail call on December 2, 1929, brought him a long, anguished letter from his mother that described in detail her great heartache at their being separated by so many miles during the Christmas season. She wrote that she would do anything if she might see him, if only for a few moments.

Checketts became very depressed by the sorrowful tone of his mother's letter, and he went to his bunk that night wishing that there existed some means by which he might establish instant communication with his mother and somehow relieve at least a portion of her grief.

At last he fell asleep. Then, after only a few minutes of deep slumber, he came wide awake with the driving compulsion that he had to go somewhere in a hurry.

Checketts got out of his cot, looked over at his buddy in the next bunk, then was startled to see his own physical body still lying on the cot beneath the draped mosquito netting.

Only momentarily shocked by the sight of his physical self lying asleep on his bunk, Checketts was more impressed by the deep awareness that he had to get moving, that he had somewhere important to go. As if he were receiving instructions from some invisible higher intelligence, he stepped outside the tent, raised his arms above his head, and looked up at the moon.

What occurred next, Checketts claimed, was breathtaking.

First, he said, he had a sensation of tremendous speed, as if he were toppling end over end in midair. Kaleidoscopic scenes of snow-covered mountaintops, river valleys, lakes, and vast areas of emptiness passed by so fast that they became blurred by the high speed at which his consciousness was moving.

When everything came to a stop, Checketts was still stretching his arms toward the moon, but now the moon shone over towering cliffs and snow-covered hills instead of tropical jungle.

Although he had never seen his parents' new home in Ogden, he somehow knew that the white house at the top of the hill before him was that very domicile.

He made his way through undisturbed snow to the porch of the house. His knock at the door produced sounds of movement within. When the door opened, his mother stood before him in her nightclothes.

Mother and son were overcome by the unexpected reunion, and tears flowed unchecked. She expressed concern that he was standing outside in the cold in his short-sleeved uniform, but Checketts told her he would be able to stay for only a few minutes, just long enough to let her know that he was all right.

With a farewell hug and kiss, he turned away from his mother, left the porch, and walked back down the hill. He looked back only once and saw his mother still standing in the open doorway, waving at him.

Soon the strange sensation of incredible speed once again captured him, and when Checketts was again aware of his surroundings, he was standing in front of his tent at the Marine base in Nicaragua. He went inside, got back into his bed, and awoke the next morning to find his pillow wet from tears.

More than ever, he was convinced that the remarkable journey to his mother's arms in Ogden, Utah, had been a real experience. Every detail was clearly defined in his mind, and he had been left with an exhilarating sense of personal freedom.

On December 28, mail call brought Checketts a letter from his mother that was dated December 3, the morning after the extraordinary adventure in his spiritual body. Both Checketts and his tentmate, to whom he had confided the experience, were able to read that his mother had confirmed the Christmas miracle in every detail.

*I*n the early 1970s, Clarisa Bernhardt accompanied her late husband, Russ, to Los Gatos, California, where he was performing his popular one-man show, Scrooge, In Person, as part of the gala Christmas season at the Olde Towne Theatre and Shopping Center. Clarisa, who lives today in Winnipeg, Manitoba, and is currently regarded as one of North America's best-known psychic-sensitives, remembers Los Gatos as appearing like a giant Christmas card of holiday decorations and good cheer, the very picture of holiday merriment.

One morning, she dropped by the theater where Russ was rehearsing to let him know that she would be doing a special taped interview for her radio show that day, so she might be a bit later than usual. She recalls that it was fairly early, around 8:30 A.M., and a gentle, brief morning rain shower had freshened the pines with a wonderful "Christmas" fragrance.

Puzzled to discover the front door to the theater locked, Clarisa remembered a stairway that would take her to the bell tower, where she could crawl through a window and enter the theater.

"When I reached the bell tower, I paused for a moment to enjoy the gorgeous rainbow that arched over the mountains," Clarisa said, "then I found my way in. I went through the balcony and down the stairs to the main theater area."

As she entered on the right side and crossed behind the last row of seats, she was aware that she was alone in the theater. It was quite obvious that Russ was not rehearsing at this time.

As she reached the aisle on the left, she started down toward the stage—and then she stopped, as if frozen.

"There, standing in the area just below the stage, was a beautiful lady in an off-white, eggshell-colored robe with a cowl that covered her hair and accented her lovely face," Clarisa said. "She was looking directly at me. I could see a beautiful and brilliant light around her. Her countenance was glowing, yet it did not diminish my ability to see her."

Clarisa closed her eyes, quickly blinking them, then opened them again, as if to clear her vision.

"But she was still there," she said, "still looking directly at me—but now she was also smiling at me."

Clarisa could feel the power from her eyes as she looked at her. "I knew exactly who she was," she said, "and I looked at her intently, trying calmly to observe as many details as possible. I wanted to etch her image in my memory. I was in the presence of the Holy Mother!"

And then she was gone. Clarisa estimated that the experience had occurred within one minute, though she felt suspended in time.

"To this day," she said, "I can close my eyes and instantly recall that magnificent experience and see her as if it's happening all over again."

Understandably, Clarisa said that she wishes she could have asked Mother Mary many things. "But I had not attempted to speak. I was completely overwhelmed. I had just seen Mary and been in the presence of the Holy Mother."

She also knew that the visitation was something important and significant in her life. In the weeks that followed before Christmas, Clarisa recalled that she was privileged to receive numerous mystical experiences and visions.

"One very special blessing manifested to heal a terrible ache in my heart," Clarisa said. "I was reunited with my dear son, who had been separated from me following tumultuous family events some years before. No matter how desperately I had worked to mend the situation, nothing had worked. The family rift keeping us apart had seemed impossible to change—and then almost instantly and miraculously, we were together again. It was truly a Christmas miracle. I will forever be thankful to Mother Mary for accomplishing such an 'impossible' task."

*T*ammie Bissonnette knew that she would have a difficult delivery because the child was breeched within her womb. But she felt that the fact that her daughter would be a Christmas baby would be ample compensation for her discomfort.

"That was before the contractions began," she recalled. "Halfway through the delivery, I would have been happy to have settled for a Valentine's Day child." Putting the birth off until February seemed, in the moment, like a good idea.

Her family doctor, Dr. Rubenstein, had debated whether or not they should take the baby through cesarean section, but after discussing the dilemma with some of his colleagues, he decided that it would be better to wrestle with the breech problem in the delivery room. Tammie would not be anesthetized, because she, the mother, would have to help. She would be given only a mild painkiller.

"I knew all these things, and I believed that I was prepared mentally and physically for the ordeal," Tammie said. "According to my calculations, my daughter, Liza, was due around the twentieth to the twenty-fifth—but then the worst happened. My water broke on the fifteenth. My husband, Phil, was out of town on business until the seventeenth, and Dr. Rubenstein had taken an early holiday and wouldn't be back until the nineteenth."

As her mother, Carla Ackerson, drove her to the hospital, Tammie kept hearing Dr. Rubenstein's caveat: "Little Liza is due to enter the world right around Christmas Eve, just when you were praying for her arrival. Of course, only Liza knows for certain when she will arrive. Doctors can only guess."

She knew that Dr. Rubenstein had intended to be back in time for the delivery, but as he had reflected, only the baby knew for certain when her birthday would be. And, of course, Phil would be crazy with worry that he wasn't there, Liza being their first child and all.

Dr. Marisse Walker, the pediatrician with whom Dr. Rubenstein had discussed the complications of the delivery in the event that something should prevent his being there, was in the midst of a difficult surgery when they arrived. Mrs. Ackerson and Tammie were informed that she absolutely could not be disturbed.

"I am afraid that the doctor summoned to pinch-hit was not the best example of the devoted practitioner," Tammie recalled. "He seemed hardly interested in hearing the nurse's summary of the difficulty of the delivery, and he was certainly indifferent toward alleviating any of my pain."

As the dilation was nearing completion, the agony was nearly driving Tammie out of her mind, and she squeezed her mother's hand so hard she feared she would snap a couple of finger joints.

"Maybe it was the terrible pain," Tammie said. "Maybe that was what made me feel like I was whirling around the room like a propeller on an airplane. I seemed to go faster and faster . . . and then—pop! I, that is, the real me, was suddenly floating above the bed in the labor room looking down on my body, my mother, and the nurse who was trying to ease my pain."

Tammie was shocked to see how contorted her facial features were. "I thought I must have died, but then my body on the bed below threshed wildly and let out an awful cry of pain," she said. "I was baffled. That was me, Tammie Bissonnette, down on the bed, but it was also me—or some aware aspect of myself—up near the ceiling watching the scene below and feeling absolutely no pain at all."

That was when she became aware that lovely Christmas music was swirling all around her.

"I heard what I thought at first was an orchestra playing 'Hark the Herald, Angels Sing,' but then I realized it was a melody only similar to that old hymn. When I heard a magnificent choir singing words of praise to God, I thought for certain that this time I really had died and gone to Heaven."

Then Tammie's attention was focused once again on her body below on the bed.

"I saw the nurse measure my dilation, and she said. 'You're ready, honey! Now where is that idiot doctor?' "

The nurse left the room, and Tammie's out-of-body consciousness followed her as she walked down the hall and located the doctor. "I saw him scowl at the interruption, for he was talking with an attractive nurse and I could see that he hated to be bothered to deliver my baby."

Almost at once after viewing the doctor's distasteful scowl, Tammie was back in the bed in the labor room, moaning again with terrible pain. She wished that she could leave her body again and go back up near the ceiling where there was no hurt.

"I did flip out of my body again during the delivery," she said. "I saw my face pale and glistening with sweat . . . and then the most extraordinary thing occurred. I saw this beautiful angel approaching me, and she was leading this lovely young woman by the hand. Before my spiritual eyes, I saw that vivacious young woman appear to be transformed—to shrink, if you will—to the size of an infant. I remember that I took the baby from the angel's arms, and then I was conscious of the two of us being dragged into some kind of tunnel with a light at the end. And the next thing I knew, I was back in my body, lying back on the hospital bed, holding my baby, Liza, and everything was all right."

Tammie's mother, Mrs. Ackerson, bent over the bed and kissed the cheeks of her daughter and her new granddaughter. "Mom said that she had managed to get a hold of Phil in his hotel room, and he was wild with happiness. He would be home sometime the next afternoon."

Tammie told her mother that she had hoped that the baby would be born closer to Christmas Eve or on Christmas Day. "But I had a vision or dream or something, Mom, and I saw a beautiful angel hand over the care and nurturing of this lovely young woman to me," Tammie said. "That young woman became baby Liza. So just as we should keep the spirit of Christmas each day in our hearts, I will surely love this little Christmas season miracle of mine every day of my life."

On Christmas Day 1989, Melissa Bauer's father asked her if she wanted to go along with him when he took Grandmother Bauer home after her holiday visit with the family.

"I was thirteen that Christmas," Melissa said, "and I felt so special that Dad had asked me to ride with them and keep him company on the drive back. In years past, he would have asked my older sister Marilyn, who was home from college for the holidays. I was really surprised that he asked me, because I expected him to say that the drive back would give him a chance to catch up with Marilyn since she had been away for three months. After all, I had been around and underfoot during that period of time. But then, Dad and I hadn't communicated much either, because he was always so busy."

Melissa also looked forward to talking with Grandmother Bauer during the trip to her house.

"Grandma was a hoot, always laughing and telling jokes about what she did when she was a teenager back in the Roaring Twenties," Melissa said. "I think she kind of embarrassed Dad sometimes when she told anyone who would listen to her stories she had been a flapper who had frequented speakeasy hideaways. I swore that I would never tell anyone the family secrets— which was a fib, because those stories were too good to keep out of the widest possible circulation."

Grandmother Bauer lived in a nearby village in New Hampshire, and it took about twenty minutes to drive between the two homes.

"After we saw Grandma safely to her door and inside to her favorite chair in her living room, Dad and I headed back home—in a sudden sleet storm," Melissa recalled. "Grandma said that we should stay until the sleet let up, but Dad said that it could last all night and only get progressively worse. It was his responsibility to open up the supermarket the next morning, so he had to get home that night."

As the storm worsened and the roads became slick and treacherous, Melissa's father took his right hand very briefly off the steering wheel to pat her on the shoulder.

"I'm glad you're with me tonight," he said. "I wouldn't like to be alone in this mess."

Melissa remembered that the loving gesture from her father made her feel wonderful and wanted.

"I just felt all warm and fuzzy inside," she said. "I wanted so much to have Dad's approval and to know that I was as special to him as Marilyn had always seemed to have been. I guess it is only natural that the older child gets a bit more attention just because she arrived first on the planet, but I do admit to having had a little sliver of sibling rivalry stuck in my psyche."

And then it became obvious to her that her father was having difficulty negotiating the familiar New Hampshire hills and curves with their new coating of freezing sleet.

But these roads weren't familiar. Melissa and her father were somewhere on a very dark and winding road and sliding backward.

"Where are we, Dad?" Melissa asked, not recognizing the area.

"I . . . I took a shortcut," he explained. "Thought it would be safer on this old road. No one travels it much any more."

Melissa remembered how she began thinking that they could slide into the ditch and not be found on the lonely stretch of road for days.

Her father was attempting to appear very calm and confident, but she knew his mannerisms too well not to recognize that he was extremely nervous and uncertain.

"Melissa, please, roll down your window and watch very carefully that I don't get too close to the edge," he asked. "I . . . think it could be quite a drop-off around here. Can't tell in the dark, of course. But I have driven this old road in daylight; I think I remember some pretty good drop-offs along this stretch. Just keep a really sharp eye."

Melissa rolled down the window and saw by the illumination from the car's back-up lights that their rear wheels appeared to be on the very edge of the gravel. She had no idea how much control her father had on the slick road, but he appeared to have managed to stop the car from sliding.

"Don't back up another inch, Dad," she shouted. Her face was stinging from the sleet and the cold, but she felt strangely exhilarated by the precarious situation.

"I was needed," she said. "Dad and Mom had always taken such good care of me, but that night, Dad really needed my help. He couldn't see clearly out the rear window that was coated with freezing sleet. And he wouldn't dare get out of the car to check for fear it would slide away from him. He really needed me to watch for the edge of the road."

In the dim light from the dashboard, Melissa could see that her father was sweating heavily, even with the open window letting in the cold.

"I'm going to release the brake and carefully accel-erate," he said, explaining his plan of action. "I hope we're on a patch of gravel where we can find enough traction to allow me to stop sliding backward and to move forward up this hill. If I can do that, we will be home free—I know it! There's an old covered bridge just over the top and then it's downhill all the way."

Melissa offered her encouragement. "Go for it, Dad."

"Easy now," he said, "I'm going very easy. Keep watching the edge, honey."

Melissa's face was numb from the cold and the sleet, but she kept looking out the window.

"That's when I saw directly behind us and just above us a brilliant white light with a bluish center," she recalled. "I don't know where it had come from. It hadn't been there moments before—and then there it was. It was strangely beautiful, and it appeared to move higher, then lower, as if it were somehow intelligently surveying our dilemma.

"I didn't hear a voice," Melissa said, "but I knew that I was receiving a message from the light that told me not to worry, that Dad and I would be all right. Somehow that light and I were connected in some mysterious and glorious way."

Melissa's father released the brake and gently pressed on the accelerator—but to his alarm, the car began sliding backward.

"Melissa, I can't control the car," he said, unable to keep the panic from his voice. "I'm sorry. We're sliding backward. Hold on, honey, we could go in the ditch and tip over. Be sure your seatbelt is buckled!"

She tried to calm her father, to tell him not to be frightened. She knew that somehow the mysterious light was in control and that they would not be harmed.

The car went backward all the way to the base of the hill, and Melissa saw the light spin off into a clump of trees, then either disappear or blink out in the darkness.

"We hadn't sat there very long when a highway patrol car pulled alongside of us," Melissa said. "The officers told us that we shouldn't try to travel up the hill. The old covered bridge had collapsed and passage would be impossible. There was nothing left up there but some broken and rotted planks and a long drop into the river. Up ahead, though, they said, was a road that would lead us back to the main highway where crews had already applied salt and sand to the slickest places."

The remainder of the drive back home was uneventful. Melissa's father praised her for being so helpful, for keeping an eye on the edge of the road, and for paying no mind to the cold and sleet that he knew had to be stinging her face.

"I had truly bonded with my father that Christmas Day," Melissa said, "but I had also bonded with something incredibly mysterious that represented a source of strength outside of myself that has returned time and again in my memory to give me courage during some very dark moments.

"I don't know if that light was an angel or an unknown intelligence of some kind. And I don't know why I felt so much a part of it. All I know for certain is that whatever it was, it became the Christmas miracle that probably saved my dad and me from injury or worse during that sleet storm."

*D*ave Bennett was recently diagnosed with Stage 4 lung and bone cancer. The cancer in his spinal column has already gnawed away at the top three discs. This kind of deterioration causes excruciating pain—add to that difficulty breathing, nausea, weakness, and debilitating tiredness from intensive chemotherapy treatments and radiation, and it becomes difficult to feel much other than agony and despair. The doctors are unable to tell Dave just how long he might expect to live. He and his wife, Cindy, are looking at an optimistic ten-year plan, yet are getting his affairs in order. That tells you something about them.

Cindy said they have had a deluge of well-meaning people offering suggestions for various techniques to try to recover. "Suggestions range from jumping up and down on a trampoline to drinking a healing Essiac Tea and all kinds of things in between," she shared. Confirming Dave would definitely not be trying the trampoline cure, she added that he does have a strong personal connection with Spirit and is able to sift through suggested cures and take what works best for him.

Dave is not afraid to die. He has done that already. In fact his near-death experience completely transformed and redirected his life many years before. While out at sea, working on a research vessel, Dave suffered an agonizing death of slowly drowning after being tossed about like a rag doll in a raging storm. He described the pain of being submersed and tossed about in dark, murky salt water with lungs near bursting and burning in need of a crucial breath of air. Just as the pain intensified to an overwhelming degree, it suddenly reverted and began to fade a little at a time until it was completely gone. Then everything went cold and dark—a cold darkness. That was how Dave described the event.

The rest of the experience is nearly the classic near-death account—of a gradual light becoming so bright and warm and full of love that one has no desire to ever leave it. Being one with the light and its love, without a physical body and no pain, suddenly other "light beings" came toward him. Dave felt he knew them and they knew him as they were supporting and helping him to adjust.

Then, before he was able to communicate with any of them, he experienced a "life review" where every minor and major thing he had said, done, and thought, and how it had affected the lives of those around him when he was alive, flashed before him. Supernaturally, he was able to review the feelings of others as the result of his actions—all the joy, happiness, heartache, disappointment, love, hurt, sorrow, grief —but all without the accompanying guilt or judgment. All the subtle interactions of his entire life were ineffably experienced. He knew the review was shown him not to be judged, but to learn and grow from.

"It felt like coming home," Dave said. "I experienced a love and acceptance like I had never felt before." Then others seemed to join the first group that had surrounded him, and Dave began to see things that were not familiar to him at all. The "others" remained supportive, but Dave felt disoriented. He thought he was looking into his future!

The clearly audible words, "This is not your time, you must return," interrupted with a bang. Like a cannon, shooting him back to his earthly body, then again, "This is not your time, you have a purpose!" Dave described the fact of "having to return" as a more painful contrast to the love and peace than the actual pain of drowning. All of this seemed to be a prelude to a miracle that was to occur on Christmas 2000.

This would be the first Christmas that Cindy would not be with the rest of her family in thirty-nine years, and she was feeling the pangs of self-inflicted guilt for not making a six-hour drive to spend even a few hours with them. Exposing Dave to any cold or flu germs could be fatal, as both radiation and chemotherapy deplete the white blood cells, thereby severely compromising the immune system of the patient.

Although she probably could have made the drive by herself, it didn't feel right leaving Dave home alone on Christmas. Even though many of the out-of-town family would have already left, Cindy planned to make the drive alone, the day after Christmas, depending on how Dave felt. She did not yet know there was likely a "higher power" at work in the decision to stay home.

Around 5 P.M. the phone rang. On days she wasn't working, Cindy says she screens calls, as they would normally be clients calling to schedule appointments, but this time she picked up the phone right away. "Hi Cindy" said the unidentified voice. It took a few seconds before Cindy recognized the voice as that of a sweet massage therapist she knew that specialized in Tai massage. "Have you ever heard of Padre Pio?" she asked. Cindy acknowledged that she had visited Padre Pio's church when she was traveling in Italy.

Padre Pio, born into a hard-working farming family in southern Italy in 1887, entered the novitiate of the

Capuchin Friars at the age of fifteen and was ordained a priest in 1910. In 1918, the five wounds of Christ's crucifixion appeared on his body, and continued to do so until his death in 1968, making him the first stigmatized priest in the history of the Church. His entire life was marked by long, arduous prayer, continual austerity, and ineffable suffering, both physical and mental as observed by those who knew him. Hundreds of thousands of devotees flock to his place of entombment in the crypt of Our Lady of Grace Church and claim spiritual and physical healings by the grace of his saintly suffering. Last year the claim of 7 million pilgrims visiting Padre Pio's mountaintop sanctuary was second only to the number of visitors to the Marian sanctuary of Lourdes, France. Padre Pio was only recently beatified as a saint by Pope John Paul II.

Even though Cindy had visited the holy site it was interesting to hear of the other woman's experience. The therapist, whose name was Nancy, continued to talk about Padre Pio. Known for his compassion and healing, it was also reported that he bilocated or was in two places at one time, the woman said. It is documented that during the Second World War, the U.S. Army air force was going to accidentally bomb an area that was occupied by allies, unbeknown to them. The fighter pilots reported seeing a monk appearing in midair, right in front of their plane, motioning for them to turn back. The fighter pilots were so frightened by the sight that they did turn back, and the impending bombing massacre was averted!

Cindy said, "She then asked me if I had heard about the healing miracles that happened around a glove that had belonged to Padre Pio."

Cindy had not, so the woman on the phone offered to put another woman who was there with her on the phone to explain. "The woman had a very sweet and calming voice and turned out to be a local television personality, but wishes to remain anonymous, so we refer to her as our 'Christmas angel,' " Cindy continued.

She told of a priest who used to be a custodian of Padre Pio's in Italy, but returned to his former parish in Brooklyn, New York, following Padre Pio's death. The priest had been given two of the gloves that Padre Pio wore on his hands to keep the blood from the Stigmata wounds from dripping on the floor. The gloves are considered sacred objects and are known for their healing properties. There were many stories of how parishioners of this Brooklyn church had miraculous healings by the gloves, which are said to give off an uncannily beautiful rose scent. The scent is always present, although emanating stronger at times, and weaker at others.

The priest kept one glove for himself and gave the other one to his sister, who felt it should be made available to all to benefit from. His sister felt that the parking-lot attendant of the church, who knew everyone in the parish, would be the best guardian for disseminating the healing power of the glove. The glove is kept in a box with a piece of a sheet that came from Padre Pio's bed, a book in which people write to Padre Pio, and one of those double-image pictures of Padre Pio that changes as you tilt it from side to side. Continuing, she interrupted herself with a little laugh and an aside, saying the parking-lot booth used to be a shrine to Frank Sinatra, until Padre Pio's box arrived. Now it is shared—Frank Sinatra and Padre Pio!

Telling of a long waiting list for the glove, the woman on the other end of the phone said that her name came up for Christmas Eve, so she felt there was no better way she could spend her own Christmas other than to share it with whoever was in need. She had the glove for two entire days, so it was still in her possession and the English massage therapist friend had mentioned Dave's cancer, wondering if he might want to touch the glove.

Dave was not feeling up to making the trip to Brooklyn, so this wonderful woman offered to come to see them.

"Now to tell you where we live, it is known as Windy Hill," Cindy said. "Our place used to be a cross country ski resort on top of a high hill that is often buffeted with lake-effect snow, and we were having a very bad blizzard that day. Since it was Christmas Day, the landlord was out of town, so the driveway had not been plowed. We were literally snowed in, yet she offered to come to us!"

At the woman's insistence, Cindy gave her directions and over an hour and a half later, via cell phone guidance, she arrived covered with snow and bearing a canvas tote.

"We sat in our living room and she pulled out a wooden box with a little picture of Padre Pio on the top," Cindy said. "She gently opened it and took out the picture that was in the box, then a little book, then very gently brought out the glove. At first I was surprised. It was a little tiny brown glove with no fingers in it. It looked like a glove you would see on a homeless person. The funny thing to me was that it was so simple. You would think it would be ornate or at least a little bigger! Padre Pio was a large man. I remembered seeing his slippers when I saw his monk cell in Italy. They were so big!"

The little brown glove had a simple metal cross gently sown onto the top side. Later, when Cindy turned it over, she saw that someone had sown a tiny piece of cloth with a little x in the place that must have been where the hand wound from the stigmata was.

"The amazing thing to us was the aroma that came from it. Anyone who smelled this rose scent could tell you that it is like no other rose smell you had ever smelled," Cindy continued. "You couldn't create it even with the best of oils or perfume!"

Dave and Cindy described the sheet from Padre Pio's bed as having the same scent, as well. It was kept in a little plastic bag, but the glove itself was not in any container, other than the box. Dave put the glove in his hand and Cindy said you could actually see the calm come over him.

Dave explained what he felt as he held the glove in his hand: "At first, I just sensed a type of love similar to what I feel when I touch my near-death experience. When I touched the glove I was feeling with my heart and not my mind. I could feel my heart opening up and feeling that light and love. I could feel both Spirit and human emotion because it was a vast amount of unconditional love. It was like going back into the light a little bit, not all the way. In order to come back from a near death you have to accept that light back. And I have been having trouble keeping my heart open and working with my light and love because of the physical fatigue and drug induced emotions. But as I stroked the glove it felt like some of the barriers were just melting away and the light in my heart was just able to open and shine as bright as ever. Well, I could just say that my spirit was singing. Spirit gets in this joyous frame of not mind—but Spirit. When

Spirit is joyous, it feels like a song in your heart and it interacts with your human emotions. It just brings tears to my eyes. It gets you a little choked up. You can feel it emanate throughout your entire body. It isn't just your heart that expands, it expands through the entire body—physically, I could feel it!"

The fact that Dave could "feel" the glove was the first hint of the miracle. Dave sat there stroking the glove as their new friend and Christmas angel told the story of the glove in more detail and described how she happened to end up with it. Dave had permanent nerve damage in the hand that could now "feel" the glove. He had not had any sensation in it for over six months!

The woman described how Padre Pio was said to bring so much compassion and insight into his parish confessional that it seemed to aid people in knowing just exactly what it was they needed to confess and release.

"The funny thing was, that it felt to me, like a little confession of my own—as I held the glove," Dave said. He found himself talking about his near-death experience, the cancer, and what it was like having it.

"As she was telling about Padre Pio's confessionals from the heart, I felt compelled to confess feelings that had welled up within me, but that I hadn't realized were there," Dave explained.

Cindy said when Dave handed the glove to her, she could immediately feel energy coming from the center of it. She felt an indescribable peace. As she handed the glove back to Dave, she took out the piece of sheet from the little bag and was amazed by the rose scent that came from it.

As Dave continued to share his feelings, the scent of roses grew stronger and stronger until the entire room was filled with the powerful rose scent and with a pervading sense of peace and love.

After tea and cookies, the Christmas angel was on the phone calling the next person with whom she was about to share the glove, telling them that she was on her way.

Later that night in bed, Dave told Cindy he could still smell the potent smell of roses. Cindy no longer smelled them until she reached over and touched Dave's hand. Then suddenly through the physical connection with him, the scent became vivid to her, as well. Cindy said she promptly fell asleep and "missed out" on the rest of Dave's miracle.

Dave said the rose scent, still strong, seemed to envelop and maintain him in this peaceful, blissful state. He drifted off to sleep, in a more relaxed state than he could remember in a very long time.

Then, he said, at 2 A.M. he was awakened to the smell of roses. That scent had become even stronger. It was everywhere and so overwhelming that he started to cry.

"I could feel my heart fully open, and I could feel my light and my spirit shining as bright as in my near-death experience. So, I got up and meditated and just enjoyed taking that energy in," Dave said.

It was as though Dave had a spiraling of energy that brought together the elements of his life into a clearer focus and design—of a ministry helping others to know of and to experience this state of grace. Somehow, his near-death experience seemed like the groundwork, the background, to a tapestry woven in anticipation of a Christmas miracle that continues to add golden threads of wonder to the mystery cloth of life itself. Holding the glove of Padre Pio reconnected Dave with the inner peace and love he had touched in his near-death experience, that had been blotted out by pain and medication, troubles and worries.

"Spirit indicated this was to be my future path—working with others who are suffering with a terminal illness. I know it is time to communicate what I have experienced and learned, and now I am using it to cope with my own terminal illness. I am to begin to share it in a more public way," Dave said.

Cindy and Dave are hopeful and prayerful that Dave will be completely healed. Dave said he believes that we all have obstacles and experiences that we must overcome and learn from so that we can evolve and grow.

"God hasn't abandoned us when things seem tough. It is necessary to see the positive and negative in all I've experienced in order to grow. God's light and love is a part of each of us and we don't have to go searching for it. We just need to open up to it," Dave said.

Even if Dave is not completely healed, Cindy and Dave feel his cancer has brought about a situation that is allowing both of them to come back to their spiritual center. That, in itself, is a wonderful gift.

When Dave went to his oncologist for the first checkup since just before Christmas, his X rays showed a miracle truly had taken place on the physical level as well. Dave's tumor had become stabilized. It was no longer growing.

"We recognize our Christmas miracle as a sign that miracles do happen and that people like our Christmas angel are around to bring miracles to us and everyone else on a daily basis," Cindy said. "We are reminded that Angels don't always have wings—sometimes they appear in a snow-covered coat and scarf!"

Padre Pio said, "Love is the first ingredient in the relief of suffering." It is clear that Padre Pio's love is continuing to touch many lives.

As an epilogue, Cindy said that in talking with their Christmas angel on the phone recently, the woman shared how deeply she herself had been touched by simply being the "courier of the glove." In addition, she learned of two more Christmas miracles with the glove after it left the Bennetts' home:

When the Christmas angel arrived at the home of the next recipient, the friend who had the tumor was unable to be present. So they called her on the phone, and while holding the glove, they all prayed for healing. In utter amazement, when the woman with the tumor went to the doctor, he declared the tumor was gone! The doctor had no way of explaining this miraculous disappearance, but the woman herself knew . . . Padre Pio's glove had healed again!

The other healing that day was that of a woman who suffered greatly with double vision. After holding the glove, she was immediately blessed with no more double vision! She was so overjoyed she was afraid to tell anybody, Cindy said, for fear the problem would return. As of now, it has not, so she has been telling everybody!

*S*herry's mom, Lorraine Lippold, was no stranger to hospitals. Many years of intense pain from scoliosis of the spine and nerve and disc problems resulted in a series of operations that would have been difficult for a young healthy person to endure, much less a woman in her seventies. Surgeons implanted metal rods in her back, from the base of her spine to her neck, that required grafting bone from the hip and leg to use in attaching the rod to the spine. This extremely complicated and dangerous surgery was performed not just once—but multiple times! For various reasons, the rods were taken out, then others reinstalled.

Enduring a body cast for six months after several surgeries, and allowing for the healing of the bone grafts, muscles, and nerves, Lorraine found the ordeals were taking a toll on her physical stamina, as it would

85

on anyone's! They still weren't right, so yet another surgery, taking out the old rods and installing rods of a more recent technology, seemed successful. Then, over a year's time of healing and more body casts, she was able to wear a plastic cast that enabled her more freedom of movement.

While unpacking boxes in a new home, Lorraine was standing on a ladder, putting some dishes in a high cupboard, when she lost her balance and fell onto a metal serving platter in the box beneath her, which sliced her leg in a manner that looked more like a shark attack than a fall. More than half of her calf was sliced to the bone, and as if that wasn't enough, the severe fall threw out the rods in her spine. She would eventually have to go in and have all the rods removed, once more, still another major back operation.

But that would be after the long, arduous process of mending and healing from the injured leg. Infections and swelling caused major problems and pain, nearly unbearable, but Lorraine pulled through, only to be dealt other onslaughts, of lupus disease and some rare form of lung disease to boot. So over many years, she was on massive doses of antibiotics and various medications for the swelling and pain. People around her marveled at her courage and stamina.

She had just begun to gain her strength back when pneumonia moved in, not once but four times! A period of two months saw her hospitalized three times with pneumonia so serious, they weren't sure she would pull through. Each time, Sherry's dad, Paul Lippold, rarely left Lorraine's side. He would sit by her hospital bed day and night, holding her hand and deep in prayer. Their faith pulled them both through one close call after another. Lorraine, a short and petite Swede, was now confined to a wheelchair full time. The surgeons did not want to risk reinstalling the rods in her spine after having to remove them after her horrendous fall. Paul would wheel Lorraine into the kitchen/family room area to the table where they would sit and read, eat, and watch television. On this one particular day, Paul noticed that Lorraine was somewhat listless and kept slumping way down in her chair.

"I'd pull her back up and arrange the pillows, setting her straighter, only to notice a short time later she would be all slumped down again," he explained. Finally, Lorraine said her back was really hurting her and she thought she would just go and stretch out in bed, so Paul wheeled her back to the bedroom and tucked her in, then went back out and watched something on television for about an hour, before going back to check on her.

When he walked into the bedroom, he heard what sounded like the noise Lorraine made while reaching the last few drops in a glass with a straw. One of the side effects of lupus is a dry mouth, so she almost always had a glass of water, ginger ale, or some liquid in a glass with a straw. He started to head right back to the kitchen to retrieve her another glass of juice, when he realized that his ears heard one thing, but the quick glance as he headed toward the bed told him another.

Realizing Lorraine was asleep, so the "gurgle sound" must not be a hint that her glass was empty, he did a fast U-turn and returned to the bedroom. As he got closer, he could tell that noise was coming from her chest! Paul tried to awaken Lorraine, even resorting to shaking her, as he got no response. After several unsuccessful attempts, he frantically called 911.

"Everything arrived at once," Paul said. "The fire department, the police, and the ambulance. The entire townhouse was filled with emergency medical personnel and they were all doing their best to revive her, but had no response. When I heard one of them yell 'bag her,' I was terrified, thinking that meant they were to bring in the coroner's bag! Of course, it didn't, and they put a tube down her throat and rushed her to the hospital."

"There in the emergency room, they worked on her, and then needed to put her in an intensive care unit, but there wasn't a single one available. So Valley Lutheran Hospital, where she was, called the same ambulance that brought her from home to the hospital

to transport her to Mesa Lutheran Hospital's intensive care unit. Lorraine was on total life support for
more than three days, when neurology scheduled an
encephalogram to determine the extent of brain damage. There was no knowledge of exactly how long Lorraine had been 'out' before they put her on life support,
but it was a consensus that, more than likely, if she ever
came around, she would be a vegetable," Paul added.

Sherry and Brad were scheduled to lecture and give
a seminar in Florida, when shortly before they were to
leave, came the first phone call that Lorraine was in the
hospital. In prayer and turmoil, they were uncertain if
they should cancel and get right to Arizona. Although
Mom had pulled through so many terrible ordeals, this
one sounded most serious. Then came the dreaded
phone call from Sherry's dad that if she wanted to see
her mother, she had better get out to Arizona immediately, as it looked like the Lord had finally called her
home. It was Mom Lippold's request not to be kept alive
by machinery and life support, and her wishes regarding
such a situation had been made clear.

After many discussions on the phone with nurses
and doctors and Sherry's dad, Brad and Sherry cancelled their Florida lecture and made plans to immediately go to Mom Lippold's bedside in Arizona. Sherry
was finding this to be an extremely difficult situation to bear. Thinking miracles do occur even under

extraordinary circumstances, she didn't think they should "pull the plug" and was shocked to learn that was about to happen, even though it was at her own mother's request.

Both Sherry and Brad had lost close family members at Christmas. Sherry's son, Erik; Brad's dad, Erling; and now—Sherry's mom. They would, of course, respect her wishes, and they made arrangements to make the trek from Iowa to Arizona. So, once again, not long before Christmas, Sherry and Brad began bracing themselves for what was beginning to look like another sad Christmas of losing a beloved family member.

The Lippolds' faith carried them through one crisis after another, yet Sherry knew this was going to be more difficult than she could imagine for them. They had been extremely active in their church, and now the prayers of their pastor, church members, friends, family, and other churches around the country were a strong support.

"This time, she must have been covered in so much prayer that it was a shield that blanketed her, keeping her safe for the three days she was—for all practical purposes and by definition—dead," Paul said, then recalling that a miracle of miracles had occurred.

Paul went home at the insistence of the nurses to take a shower and get at least a couple of hours of sleep, before returning to the hospital. When he came back, he thought he was seeing things as he walked into Lorraine's room and there she was sitting up in the hospital bed, reading the paper!

In just a few hours' time, she had come out of the coma, shocking the entire hospital staff! To everyone's utter amazement, just minutes before they were about to remove the life-support, a nurse who was checking on Lorraine had affectionately stroked her hand, and then holding on to it for a second, had noticed what she thought was a response from Lorraine.

The nurse screamed out that she could feel a slight squeeze back from the patient . . . so suddenly, hospital staff went right to work on her and, miraculously, she came around—and out of the coma!

After reviewing the situation again and again, all reiterated that Lorraine's coming out of the coma was stunning enough, but the fact that she demonstrated no signs of any neurological damage was something of a miracle.

Instead of another Christmas funeral, Sherry and Brad celebrated Christmas with Lorraine, who was still weak from the ordeal but gaining in strength daily, and the rest of the family. They were shown, once again, that even when the odds are "stacked against you"—as they surely seemed to be with all that Lorraine had been through—miracles can and do happen. A better Christmas gift, Sherry and her dad could not have had!

When Bernadette Lopez was a schoolgirl in Las Cruces, New Mexico, she contracted polio, which she remembers as a disease that made her burn with fever and left her right leg paralyzed and her left leg painfully twisted.

"My father or my mother had to carry me back and forth to my bed from the toilet or other rooms," Bernadette said. "My mother was so worried about me that she would sometimes sleep with me in case I needed something during the night."

The disease had quite understandably left Bernadette very depressed. "I was not yet ten years old, and the doctors told my parents that I would probably never walk again. Later, I might try leg braces and crutches, but a wheelchair would be a more likely prognosis. And along with that grim malediction came my inner sadness that I would never be a wife or a mother or have any kind of normal life—ever."

On Christmas Eve 1942, Bernadette's father had bundled her up so that she could attend mass with them. They were very poor in those days, and since most of the little money that her parents did manage to save went for Bernadette's medicines, there were few presents for her baby sister, Rosa; her parents; or herself.

"Mother said that the most important thing was that we had each other and could be together on Christmas Eve," Bernadette recalled.

Then, after they had returned from mass and had a little bit to eat, Bernadette suddenly began to run a high fever.

"Perhaps the chilly night air had affected me adversely or the night had been filled with too much excitement for me," Bernadette said, "but I was soon shivering and moaning incoherently."

In order to save on their electricity bill, Bernadette's mother would often crawl into bed with her and read to her by the light of a candle that she would set on a bedside chair. Although her husband warned her of the potential danger of such a practice, she felt that the reading of a special Christmas story would bring some cheer to their crippled daughter.

Bernadette said that she doesn't remember at all what her mother was reading to her that night. Her fever was very high, and to her nine-year-old mind, she was dying.

"When I came back to periods of semiconsciousness, I was glad that Mama was there with me," Bernadette said. "But most of the time I had no idea where I was or who was with me."

Sometime that night, Bernadette's fevered dreams became a kind of waking night vision, and she was startled to find that she was somehow out of her body and that her conscious self was floating up near the ceiling. Below her, she could see her shivering body and her mother's familiar form on the bed—and then she was astonished to see two columns of angels standing at the sides of her bed. She remembers clearly that there were six of the glorious beings on her right side and six on her left. "They began to sing the sweetest, most beautiful song that I had ever heard," Bernadette said. "And all around them was the most magnificent music being played by an unseen orchestra. I thought to myself, truly, this is the song that the shepherds had heard on high on the Christmas Eve when Christ was born."

But the angels began to sing louder and louder, until their mighty chorus of voices hurt her ears. And the angelic beings themselves appeared to grow larger and larger as they sang louder and louder.

Just as the song of the angels seemed to reach a cre-
scendo, Bernadette awakened to the horror of discover-
ing that she and her mother were enveloped in flames.

The girl jumped out of bed and dragged her mother
from the flames that had engulfed them.

"I pulled my unconscious mother away from the
burning bed," she remembered, "and then I began
beating out the flames, first with my bare hands, then a
bath towel. The bedclothes were badly burned, as well
as half the mattress and one of the pillows."

Her father appeared at the door of her bedroom
and shouted a combination of alarm and joy: "Bernadette! You are walking! The bed is on fire!"

The miracle of it all had not struck her until her
father had shouted it aloud. How could she, a small
girl weakened by fever and paralysis, have managed to
jump out of bed and pull her mother to safety?

Although Bernadette has asked herself that question now for nearly sixty years, she always arrives at the
same answer: It could only have been due to the twelve
beautiful angels who appeared at her bedside on that
Christmas Eve in 1942 and accomplished four miracles.

"First, they performed a miracle of healing on my
legs," she said. "Then they kept singing louder and
louder until I awakened to save my mother and myself
from the fire that had begun when Mama had fallen

asleep and knocked over the candle. The third miracle was that although Mama's dressing gown and night-dress were burned off her body on her left side and my nightgown was scorched black, neither of us had the slightest burn on our flesh.

"Fourth, and the greatest Christmas miracle of all, I continued walking without assistance. I was a bit unsteady at first, but my parents never had to carry me anywhere again. Within a couple of months, I was once again running and skipping rope with my friends, a happy schoolgirl who would never forget the angels from on high and their beautiful song of healing.

"I know that those same angels have watched over me all of my life," Bernadette said, concluding her story, "and from time to time, I have been very aware of their presence around me. And, oh, yes, I married when I was twenty-three years old, and I had three wonderful, healthy children, two of which have made me a grand-mother four times. My Christmas miracle demolished the doctors' malediction that I would spend my life in a wheelchair."

*W*hen the doctors pronounced their solemn recommendation in March 1993 that Russell Miller should be allowed to die in peace, his family rallied and vowed that he would be up and singing Christmas carols with them in December.

There was no question that the prognosis appeared very disheartening. From the medical perspective, recovery was impossible.

The fifty-three-year-old Miller had entered a coma after an aneurysm burst in his brain, and the specialists at the Colorado hospital held out no hope of his ever regaining consciousness. Although they understood what a difficult family decision they had placed before the Millers, they solemnly offered their best advice that Russell's feeding tube should be unplugged and he be permitted to die peacefully.

Kathy Ebert, Miller's twenty-six-year-old daughter, remembered vividly the shock that their family received that snowy afternoon in early March when their longtime family physician, Dr. Roberts, grimly concurred with the specialists.

"Dad and Doc Roberts had been friends for years," Kathy said, "and he had tears in his eyes when he said that there was little or no hope that Dad would ever come out of the coma. And if he ever did, Doc told us, he would be on the level of a vegetable—and he would probably never be able to recognize any of us ever again. As much as it gave him sorrow, Doc Roberts suggested that we strongly consider the specialists' advice to allow Dad to pass on."

At that point, Kathy recalled, her mother, Maureen, put her arms around Kathy and her brother, twenty-two-year-old Randy, and with a trembling voice and tears streaming down her cheeks, told them that it had to be a family decision. She alone would not—could not—be the one to pass judgment on whether their father would live or die.

Randy wiped his eyes on a handkerchief and took a deep breath, as if to fix his resolve, before he spoke: "The specialists said there is little or no chance that Dad will ever regain consciousness. Well, if there is even the slightest chance that he can wake up and live, how can we deny him that possibility? Even if it is a million or two million to one, it's still a chance, isn't it?"

Kathy and Maureen became very still, as if mentally pondering the odds. Would it be fair to Dad—or to any of them—if he simply lay there in a coma for months and months before they finally gave in to the specialists' recommendation and allowed him to die?

But Randy wasn't finished with his argument. "We've always been a praying and a Bible-reading family," he reminded his mother and sister. "We've always put our trust in God. I say we keep on praying until He cures Dad. I say we just keep on focusing on seeing Dad home with us celebrating Christmas! Dad has always loved Christmas so much. With the help of God, let's create a Christmas miracle!"

Kathy nodded her agreement. They made a pact at that very moment to make a prayerful and joyful noise around their father's bed, night and day.

They made a vow to have their father home and singing Christmas carols with them in eight months.

They would practice the faith that had begun with the miraculous birth of the Christ child, and they would never stop believing that they couldn't make another miracle happen.

From that moment on, there was always at least one member of the Miller family beside Russell's hospital bed. Each day, Maureen read the Bible with great feeling, just as if her beloved husband were awake and participating in their daily family devotions.

Randy prayed aloud and placed his hands on his father's head, citing the example of Jesus laying on hands during the course of his healing ministry. A sports enthusiast since his childhood, Randy also assumed the role of a compassionate but persistent coach. He would sit beside his father's bed and repeat words of encouragement over and over, until they became a kind of chant: "Okay, Dad, come on now. I know you can hear me. Come back to us now, Dad. You can do it, Dad."

Kathy brought her guitar and accompanied herself as she sang all of her father's favorite hymns. As often as possible, she brought her ten-year-old twin daughters to sing along with her in a family trio. When her husband was able to join them, they formed a harmonious quartet that inspired the entire corridor with their joyous gospel songs.

Once a day, all the members of the Miller family—including any friends or relatives who had come to visit—would form a circle around Russell's hospital bed and clasp hands in a silent prayer for healing.

Within about ten days after the Miller family had begun their healing regimen, an amazed nurse witnessed the impossible when Russell opened one eye.

Four weeks later, he opened both eyes, and it was apparent to all those present that he was looking around the hospital room with intelligent curiosity.

The third week in April, just six weeks after an assessment of Russell Miller's burst aneurysm had led experienced medical specialists to declare that he would remain in a coma until death overtook him, he moved most of his fingers and some of his toes.

In mid-June, less than three months after he had lost consciousness, Russell Miller was responding to sounds and recognizing members of his family. He was opening his mouth and attempting to speak to his wife, children, grandchildren, relatives, and friends.

In another month, he was able to go home.

Once he was in his familiar home environment, Russell rapidly continued to improve. In a very short time, he was able to walk and speak normally. He ate meals with the family, watched television, and began to read books, magazines, and newspapers. Soon he was joining in the family's prayers for his health to be completely restored.

By that Christmas, Russell Miller was able to participate fully in his family's celebration of the holiday. His devoted wife, daughter, and son had not accepted the doctors' grim pronouncement that he was doomed to live out his remaining days in a coma. Their unyielding love, their boundless faith, and their constant prayers had petitioned the Creator to grant them a true Christmas miracle.

*I*s it possible that a mere Christmas card can engender a miraculous healing?

Dr. Franklin Ruehl, a theoretical physicist who lives in a suburb of Los Angeles, recalled an incident from 1989 involving his mother, which seems to indicate that such a miracle is indeed within the realm of feasibility.

"Mother had long suffered from chronic back pain," Dr. Ruehl said. "In fact, as long ago as 1953, an orthopedic surgeon had diagnosed her with premature arthritis of the back and predicted that it would continue to progress with an ever-increasing rate with the passage of time. As a consequence, she was always trying new exercises in an effort to combat this problem."

In early September 1989, Mrs. Florence Ruehl saw a fitness guru on television demonstrate a supposedly ideal stretching exercise for the back. Carefully, she followed along step by step with the instructor's example—but she immediately felt a bolt of pain shoot through her lower back.

"By the time I got home, I found her lying in bed, writhing in excruciating agony," Dr. Ruehl said. "Analgesics provided some measure of relief, but only temporarily. Because of her distrust of doctors, Mother adamantly refused to see a physician, but as the days dragged on, it was evident that she had more than a transient problem. Sitting upright was especially painful, so she would end up eating her meals standing at the kitchen counter."

Dr. Ruehl said that he finally got his mother to agree to visit a female chiropractor, but the erstwhile healer spent most of the time espousing the doctrine of the natural health movement, giving Florence Ruehl only a brief session of ultrasound therapy, which proved completely ineffective.

In mid-November, she relented and allowed her son to take her to a traditional medical center where, after a battery of tests, an attending physician informed them that Mrs. Ruehl hadn't fractured any vertebrae or torn any ligaments, as they had feared, but had simply pulled some muscles. The doctor went on to express surprise at how she had virtually no signs of arthritis for a woman of her age. He prescribed a two-week regimen of the powerful drug prednisone.

"It worked wonders," Dr. Ruehl recalled. "Mother got back on her feet and immediately spent as much time as possible Christmas shopping, fearing the beneficial response to the drug would wear off. It did. And the doctor refused to renew the prescription, stating his case that the potent medication could have devastating side effects if taken over a prolonged period of time. Mother once again found herself back in bed and unable to sit up as the month of December rolled around."

Dr. Ruehl began his Christmas shopping, hunting for gifts and cards. While he purchased several items and was able to accumulate a beautiful array of cards featuring cats for his mother, an ailurophile of the first order, he continued to search for an ideal card that would somehow properly address the miserable experience she was enduring with her back problem. He had canvassed all the stores in several malls but found only the standard kind of Christmas greetings.

"Then, on Christmas Eve, I happened to chance upon a small out-of-the-way card shop," he said. "I read one verse after another, finding them all bearing the traditional blissful greetings.

"Just as I was about to leave, I spotted a large, beautiful card, obscured by frolicking Santas. Reading it, I knew instantly that it was the card for which I had been searching—the very card meant specially for my stricken mother. It was as though Fate had guided me to that very shop and that very card."

When he returned home, his mother apologized for not having had a chance to get any cards for him. Dr. Ruehl then invited her to take half of the cards that he had purchased.

"I spread them out, facedown, and told her to pick cards at random that she could then give to me," he said. "Of course, I withheld that special card."

On Christmas morning, Mrs. Ruehl came out to the living room, determined to at least sit up to read her cards and to open her gifts. When she began to read the special card that her son had found for her, they both cried.

"The card had obviously been penned by someone who appreciated that not everyone at Yuletide is happy, that serious problems may be plaguing some people in this season of joy," Dr. Ruehl said.

"The verse in that precious card that began 'With all my love, Mother,' stated that although it was Christmas when everyone else may be feeling happy, it can be very difficult to smile and pretend things are all right when they really haven't been. And while there may have been times when she wondered how she could carry on, the verse proclaimed that if anyone could do it, she could—because she had always had an inner strength that would never allow her to give up.

Because of her determination, she was a very special woman who was very easy to love and she was wished a Merry Christmas so filled with love that she would never feel alone."

Incredibly, Dr. Ruehl said, after his mother read the card, she stated that she was feeling less pain when she sat up. She was able to be seated at the dining room table and enjoy their Christmas turkey dinner.

"Within the next few days, she improved at an astounding rate," he stated, "soon resuming all her normal activities. And now, twelve years later, she still has suffered no recurrence of that terrible back pain. She has, though, limited her exercise regimen to brisk walking—and she snaps off the TV anytime an exercise expert pops up."

As a scientist, Dr. Ruehl understands that skeptics might assert that his mother would have recovered eventually, that the timing of her resurgence with the reading of the card was purely coincidental. "But Mother and I are convinced that that Christmas card possessed a miraculous healing power," he said.

*J*ust before Thanksgiving, November 1990, truck driver Ray De La Cruz was sitting in his rig at an intersection in Mesa, Arizona, eager to get home after a hard five days on the road. As a line of pedestrians moved along the crosswalk in front of him, Ray glanced at his wristwatch, once again admiring the turquoise band that his wife, Renee, had given him for his fiftieth birthday in July.

Suddenly, his eyes began to cloud with a gray mist. He felt disoriented. His surroundings began to dim, and he prayed for the light to change so he could pull his rig over to the side of the road.

Within a few moments, Ray was unable to see the traffic lights, and only the sound of the horns of irritated motorists behind him told him that the light had turned green and he could drive across the intersection. Somehow he managed to pull his truck and trailer off the street just as he went completely blind.

Later, as he told his story, Ray De La Cruz admitted that he was very frightened when this terrible thing occurred. "I felt panic," he said. "I had no idea what had happened to me."

Sadly enough, neither did the specialists at the clinic.

Renee accompanied Ray when he went for a battery of tests, because he wanted her there to hear everything the doctors said and try to understand anything that he might miss in his nervousness and anxiety.

The examining doctors were able to dismiss Ray's fear of a brain tumor or any number of dire physical conditions, but they remained puzzled as to the cause of his sudden blindness.

Renee told the specialists that Ray was never sick, that he never even complained of an occasional headache. How could such a thing as this mysterious blindness occur all of a sudden?

"And I had no pain or no headache all the time when the doctors were examining me," Ray said. "I felt fine. I just couldn't see."

Finally, one of the doctors said—perhaps more in frustration than in a medical conclusion—that what was required to restore Ray's sight was a miracle.

"Mr. De La Cruz," he said, "we cannot find anything physically wrong with your eyes or anything that could have caused your sudden blindness. What we really need to restore your sight is some kind of a miracle."

Ray endured his sightlessness for three weeks before Renee declared that he had suffered enough. It was only a few days before Christmas. She would pray to Mother Mary to lift the shutters from Ray's eyes and restore his sight by the holy day of her son's birth.

"I asked Renee if she shouldn't have given the Holy Mother a little more time," Ray said, "but she argued that since the medical specialist had said that it would take a miracle to cure my blindness, then we would ask for a miracle. And every believer in miracles knows that they can happen in a split second."

Encouraged by his wife's faith, Ray began to pray also.

"And we asked our little daughters, Michele and Teresa, to pray with us until their bedtime," Ray said. "Then, after mass on Christmas Eve, from nine o'clock until eight the next morning, Renee and I said the rosary and prayed for my healing."

About eight o'clock on Christmas Day, Ray came down with a fever. "I felt like I was burning up," he said. "It seemed as though there were flames all around me. I got hotter and hotter. I felt like I had gone to Hell. I started screaming for Mother Mary to save me from the fire and the fever."

As Ray lay back on the bed, Renee placed a cool, wet cloth on his forehead.

"And then, somehow in my inner eye, I saw Mother Mary," Ray recalled. "She wore a blue gown, a white veil, and she held a rose in her right hand. She smiled at me—and then she disappeared."

When Ray told Renee that he had been blessed with a vision of the Holy Mother, she became very excited and asked Michele what time it was. She wanted to write down the exact time of the visitation so that they had a record of the marvelous event.

In spite of his blindness, Ray had continued to wear his watch due to habit. When he heard Renee ask the time, he automatically glanced down at his wrist.

"And my eyes began to focus on my watch," he said. "Within just a few moments I could clearly see the numerals on the dial and the pattern of the turquoise band. I could see!"

Overwhelmed with joy, Ray leaped from his bed and kissed and embraced his wife and daughters. He could see! Mother Mary had restored his sight. And he could feel that the fever had also left him. The Holy Mother had brought them their Christmas miracle.

Later that joyous Christmas night, Ray and his wife sat down on the sofa in the living room to think about what had just occurred. They both knew that there was a lesson in the miracle that Mother Mary had bestowed upon Ray.

"We thought for a long time," Ray said, "and then a thought came to me. My sight left me when I looked at my watch at an intersection—and it returned when Renee wanted to know what time it was that I had the vision of Mother Mary. I knew that all of this had something to do with time."

Renee and Ray thought and prayed through most of that night about the mystery of Ray's blindness and the miracle that had restored his sight—and by morning they felt they had the answer.

When Ray had been discharged from military service, he had told his parents that he didn't have "time" to go back to school. He needed a job.

As he grew older, he could not find the "time" to get married until he was in his late thirties. Although Renee was ten years younger than he, Ray kept putting off having children, insisting that it was "not yet the right time." Now Ray was over fifty, Renee was forty, and their daughters were only nine and seven. Michele and Teresa needed a father who would spend "time" with them.

Ray always complained that he didn't have "time" to help with the housework, to maintain the yard, to play with the girls, to go to church, to visit his parents—because he had to keep long hours behind the wheel of his truck. And yet he was the one who kept volunteering for the long hauls.

"To get more money to pay the bills," he said in his defense. "My time earns money."

Renee stroked her husband's hair and pulled his head to her shoulder. "And how much time do you have left with your daughters before they are grown and married?" she challenged him in a soft voice. "How much time do we have left before we are too old to enjoy one another? How much time do we have left before God calls you—or me—home? And when you are home, how much time do you waste by playing cards with your friends when you could be having quality time with the girls and me?"

Ray had no argument against such charges. He then clearly understood that Mother Mary had given him another chance to have more time with his family and the things that really mattered in life. She had taken his sight—then restored it with a Christmas miracle—so that he might truly see.

Ray De La Cruz has enjoyed full vision ever since his dramatic Christmas miracle. He quit his job driving big rigs across the country and went to work as a dispatcher for a taxi service. He is home every night for dinner, and he spends as much time as possible with his family.

And there was even a bonus to his miracle: Before he mysteriously lost his sight, he required bifocal lenses in his glasses. Since the Christmas miracle bestowed by Mother Mary, he has not needed eyeglasses at all.

*E*ach year during the Christmas holidays, we receive numerous reports from sincere men and women who tell us that they received a visit from the spirit of a departed loved one sometime during the traditional twelve days of Christmas.

Some may theorize that such visitations may be due to the power of suggestion brought on by the nostalgia for the past that is so prevalent during the Christmas season. The sights, sounds, and smells of the holiday have an incredible power to cause us to revisit cherished memories of those dear ones who have passed to the other side.

Or is it possible that the spirits of our beloved departed truly do draw nearer to us during this wonderful, yet sometimes melancholy and introspective, time of the year?

For many men and women, the holiday season can be a time of loneliness and a great longing for what they remember as much better times in their past. And for those who have lost loved ones during the Christmas holiday, a season that was once associated with joy and family togetherness can become a time of sorrow and depression. It may be that the grief of loved ones on the earthplane can draw the departed back to offer reassurance that they are all right and that life and love truly do extend beyond death.

When Joyce Epstein's twenty-four-year-old sister, Nan, and her husband, Jason Moore, were killed in an airplane crash on September 12, 1988, she felt as if she could no longer go on living.

The children of a Roman Catholic mother and a Jewish father, Joyce had been Nan's surrogate mother since she was nine and Nan was four.

"Our mother died very young of cancer," Joyce said, "and Dad didn't remarry until I was in my second year of college, so I had a lot of years of looking out for my baby sister."

In spite of the surrogate mother relationship assumed by Joyce—or perhaps, because of it—she said that the two of them had always been closer than most sisters she knew.

"It had been pretty hard after Mom died," Joyce said. "She had been a lively Irish-American girl with sparkling green eyes and coal black hair. No one could resist her charm and her good spirits, and the sound of her laughter would encourage the most solemn of stone statues to join in the fun. Before she got sick, we would sometimes as a family go to Saturday synagogue with Dad, then get up on Sunday morning to go to mass with Mom. And in December, we celebrated both Christmas and Hanukkah, placing a crèche with the baby Jesus beneath the Christmas tree and lighting the eight candles on the menorah to commemorate the miracle of the oil that fueled the candelabrum in the Temple for eight days.

"After Mom died, I more or less floated between the two faiths," she said. "Dad wasn't a strict orthodox Jew, so he let us girls pick and choose as the spirit moved us, so to speak."

Although she kept close tabs on her sister even when she was attending city college, Joyce was delighted when Nan began dating Jason Moore during their junior year in high school.

"Jason came from a good family, and he was a decent, hard-working guy himself," she said. "I had a feeling that this would be one of those high-school romances that would last forever."

Sometimes, Joyce learned to her sorrow, "forever" on Earth may not last for a very long period of time.

"Nan and Jason were such a wonderful couple," she said. "They both got jobs right out of high school and began to save for their marriage. Jason went to night school at a junior college in the city, and he was determined to better himself."

After nearly six years of hard work and planning for their future, Jason Moore and her sister decided that they could enter comfortably into marriage. They had acquired a sizable savings account, and Jason had satisfied the graduation requirements at the junior college, been promoted several times at work, and was now taking night courses at city college. Nan's position as a cashier at the bank was secure, and it now seemed as though all systems were go to continue their lifepath together as a married couple.

But the always frugal, always practical couple did not go on their honeymoon immediately after their wedding that May. They put it off until September when they knew they could better afford it after the expense of the wedding reception.

"They got married in a civil ceremony to avoid any complications with any religious issues," Joyce said. "Jason's folks were Methodists, Nan had decided to be confirmed a Roman Catholic in Mom's honor, Dad and our stepmom were Jewish, and I was sort of a New Age blend. The newlyweds hosted a really great reception at one of the local hotels—and they paid every dime of it themselves."

It was during takeoff of their honeymoon flight that the small commuter plane crashed.

"It was supposed to take them to a larger airport where they would take off for Tahiti," Joyce said. "Instead, it rose just high enough to slam back down to the ground and take Nan and Jason, seven other passengers, and the three crew members to their deaths."

Joyce Epstein entered a period of deep depression after the fatal accident.

"For a time, I sincerely did not feel that I could go on living," she stated frankly. "My sister and Jason had become my world. Shortly after Nan had graduated from high school, Dad and our stepmother had moved to a different city, leaving me, Nan's surrogate mother, to look after her. My own plans for marriage had been dashed when my fiancé was involved in a serious automobile accident and left mentally impaired. I had compensated for the loss of my future by spending even more emotional energy on Nan and Jason. I was thirty-one, and I felt as though my life was over."

Although she had sought counsel from a rabbi, a priest, her father, and certain of her friends, Joyce could find no respite from her grief. "I barely slept. And when I did, my dreams were haunted by scenes of the crash and my deep sense of loss."

Joyce is now somewhat ashamed to admit that for a time she had even considered suicide. "I felt that since Nan and Jason had been taken from me, I would join them on the other side. Thank God, I had confessed such

a plan to a priest, and he convinced me that such a dras-
tic deed would not produce the results that I desired."

Three months after the tragic deaths of her sister
and brother-in-law and between the Hanukkah and
Christmas celebrations, Joyce left her home to seek rest
and seclusion in a small ski resort in Colorado.

"There was absolutely no way that I could deal with
the holidays in the old familiar places where Nan and
I had spent so many wonderful holidays," she said, "so
I found this little out-of-the-way lodge where I could
seek solace of spirit."

One night as she sat reading near the fireplace in
her room, Joyce unmistakably felt a physical presence
behind her.

"I turned to see the images of Nan and Jason standing behind me in the center of the room," she recalled.
"I saw them as solidly as they had ever appeared in life.
They were smiling and holding hands—and for the
first time in months, I smiled, too."

Joyce is certain she actually heard Nan speaking
in her familiar, soft, lilting voice, so much like their
mother's gentle Irish brogue.

"Please do not continue to grieve so for us," Nan's
spirit told her. "Jason and I are all right. And our love
is even stronger here than it was on Earth."

Joyce tried to fight back the tears and the sudden
rush of emotion that caused her to shout: "Why did

you leave me? Why did you leave me alone? I can't go
on without you!"

Nan's lovely features seemed momentarily to be
feeling Joyce's pain, but then she smiled and spoke with
authority: "Of course you can, Sis. You know, when I
was just a little girl, there were times when you had to
leave me alone for a while. I would cry, fearing that if
something happened to you, I wouldn't be able to live
without you. But you always came back home, and we
were together again. One day, my dear sister, you will
join us here, and the three of us will be together again
with Mom and other dear ones of our family who have
already come home. Until that day, my darling, be
happy and live a life of joy and fulfillment."

Before Joyce could speak again, Nan and Jason
faded from sight—but the impact of her sister's words
have never left her.

"The proof of my sister's immortality freed me from
my deep depression," Joyce said. "And the fact that she
appeared so happy permitted me to become positive
about life once again."

Joyce concluded the story of her Christmas miracle
by stating that all of her friends were pleased to notice
her new positive attitude when she came home after
the holidays.

"To all who would listen," she said, "I told the story
of a sister's love that was able to push aside the dark

curtain of death long enough to restore the faith of one who had felt left behind to survive only in gloom and despair. To all who would listen, I declared that love is the greatest power in the universe—and maybe that is the true message of Christmas."

*T*here can't be any worse time to be fired than at Christmas. At twenty-six, Earl Burdick felt that he was a complete failure.

Four years before, in 1980, he had taken a job teaching high school English and journalism in a suburb of Chicago—a position that he hoped would serve as a stepping-stone to help him achieve his dream of becoming a full-time freelance writer. After the first semester, he learned that he was not cut out to be a disciplinarian—and facing the classrooms of unruly, disrespectful students until the end of the school year in June became a living hell.

A fellow faculty member who knew Earl was leaving teaching suggested that he sell insurance. "You can write during the day and make evening appointments to call on prospective clients after work," his friend said, making the schedule seem ideal.

But it took Earl less than a month to discover that he had absolutely no talent for intruding on tired and often irritable people and convincing them that the acquisition of an insurance policy and its subsequent payment obligations would be the answer to all their earthly concerns.

Finally, in the winter of 1981, he secured a job as the manager of a convenience store, and things seemed to be going well—so well that a year later, in the winter of 1982, he married Marjorie, the patient young woman to whom he had been engaged since their senior year in college.

Although he put in long hours at the store, he still managed to find time to write after work and on weekends, and he had received several encouraging rejection slips and had made one small sale to a trade journal. Yes, things were going so well that they decided they could afford to begin a family. Marjorie was expecting in May.

And now, two weeks before Christmas in 1984, the convenience store had been bought out by a national chain of similar marketplaces, and Earl had been summarily fired as its manager. Desperate, he had suggested his moving a couple of rungs down the ladder and working as a salesclerk, a stock boy, a custodian. But the new owners informed him that they would be bringing in their own specially trained crew to staff the store. They no longer required his services in any capacity.

It was two in the afternoon. Somehow Earl had to focus on the hard reality of becoming suddenly unemployed. After three years, he had come to rely mightily on a weekly paycheck. And now with a baby on the way. . . .

Oh, dear God, how was he going to tell Marjorie what had happened? How long could they stretch their meager savings until he found another job?

Although it was not his custom to do so, Earl walked into a bar, ordered a stiff drink, and sat down at a small table near the door. As he took a moment to survey his unfamiliar surroundings, the thought struck him that this was only the second or third time he had ever been in a bar in his life.

Earl knew that he had been walking the streets in a rather disoriented mental state, and he glanced at the address on the napkin under his drink to see where it was that he had randomly stopped his wandering and attempted to regain some perspective. Judging from the address on the soggy napkin, he had walked a lot farther than he had thought.

After Earl had sat in brooding silence for a few minutes, he was startled out of his interior monologue of despair by a well-dressed, pleasantly smiling stranger who asked if he might join him.

Glancing up and noticing that the man already had his hand resting on the back of one of the chairs at the table, Earl shrugged and indicated that he could sit down if it pleased him to do so.

"Thank you, Earl." The man smiled, sitting down opposite him.

"How do you know my name?" Earl asked.

"Oh, I know a lot about you, Earl," the stranger said. His eyes seemed sad and his voice concerned when he added, "It's difficult to adjust to cruel circumstances when you are suddenly fired, especially at Christmas, but you must not be discouraged."

Earl squinted over the edge of his glass and studied the man carefully. Rather tall, well built, salt-and-pepper hair at the temples. A soft voice that communicated quiet strength and confidence. Bright blue eyes that seemed to have the power to peer within one's soul.

"I'm sorry that I don't remember you," Earl said apologetically, extending his hand. "Where did we meet, Mr. . . .?"

The man shook Earl's hand warmly. "Oh, we've never met in person," he said, "but I know of your problem, and I want to help you. It's Christmas, your wife Marjorie is expecting your first child, and you're out of work."

Earl was feeling very uncomfortable. "You know my name, my wife's name," he began. "You know that Marjorie's pregnant. You know that I just got fired. Man, you are beginning to creep me out. Are you one of the suits from the company that just fired me? If you want to give me another job, that's fine. Maybe you suddenly got a guilty conscience over firing me at Christmas time."

The stranger smiled and denied working for the company that had acquired the convenience store and terminated Earl's position as manager. And then the man proceeded to tell him just how much he really knew about the most intimate details of Earl Burdick's life.

"I have never been so mesmerized, so enraptured in my life," Earl told us recently as he recounted the story of his Christmas miracle. "The stranger spoke in this incredibly soothing voice, and he really seemed to know everything about me and my hopes and my dreams. He knew my birth date, Marjorie's birth date, how the two of us had met in college, on and on. I just sat there and listened to him with my mouth hanging open."

And then, Earl said, came the most amazing thing of all: "He told me that he knew that what I wanted most in life was to be a writer. He told me of a small community newspaper in one of the suburbs that needed a managing editor. He wrote down the address and he told me whom to see. Then he gave me a little pep talk about how newspaper work could help me polish my skills as a writer and teach me the discipline of meeting deadlines under pressure. He told me to keep my chin up and never become discouraged. 'We never walk alone,' he said. There's always someone to reach out and give us a helping hand.'"

Earl was so heartened by the man's inspirational message and the tip on the newspaper job that it took him a moment to realize that the stranger was no longer sitting at the table speaking to him. He looked up to see him walking out the front door.

"I ran after him to thank him," Earl said, "but he must have blended right in with the people walking on the street, because he was nowhere in sight. I was right behind him, but somehow I lost him."

Before Earl called Marjorie with the bad news that he had been fired, he dialed the telephone number on the slip of paper that the stranger had given him.

"The man who answered the phone was the publisher of the community newspaper," Earl said. "He was astonished that I had called that afternoon, because his managing editor had just walked out on the job that noon and left him in a desperate situation. They had to have a special Christmas edition with the last-minute shopping advertisements out in three days. We struck an instant rapport, and I told him of my background as editor of the college newspaper, as an English and journalism teacher, and as a freelance writer. I made an appointment to see him that next morning, and I got the job as managing editor that I held for over ten years."

Earl said that at first he figured that the stranger in the bar had to be some incredible psychic or a remarkable mentalist like the Amazing Kreskin.

"I went back to the bar a few times over the next several months, thinking maybe the man might frequent the place, but I never saw him again," he said. "I tried to describe him to the bartenders who work there, but none of them claimed to recognize him at all."

Later, as Earl replayed the whole strange and wonderful episode in his mind, he came to a very different conclusion.

"No ordinary human—even if he were the world's greatest psychic—could have known all the things about me that he did," he said. "And what about giving me the name of the publisher who had just lost his editor that very day? That compassionate and remarkable stranger was no psychic—he was my own special Christmas angel!"

One of our favorite Christmas miracle stories was told to us some years ago by a woman who had grown up on a farm outside a small town in North Dakota in the 1930s.

"That December we were living in an old farmhouse that had more cracks than Daddy could patch with tar paper," Julie Wilkins remembered. "We had lost our farm the year before and we had lost Mama to typhoid fever that summer. There were four of us kids—Steve, twelve; Larry, eight; Merrie, fourteen; and I was ten—who had to nestle as close as possible to the old oil burner in the front room and try to keep warm enough to do our homework at night."

It was just before Christmas that Julie came down with a really bad fever.

"We had but one blanket a piece," she remembered, but Merrie and the boys all piled the covers on me when they were doing their chores and home-work. Normally, everyone walked around that cold and drafty old house with blankets around us like Sioux Indians, but they wanted me to get warm enough to break my fever."

After losing the family farm, their father worked during the spring, summer, and fall as a hired man for Mr. Hanson, an elderly farmer. "The problem was, old man Hanson had no need of hired help during the winter months," Julie said, "but we still had need for food. Daddy was lucky to get a part-time job at the elevator until fieldwork began in the spring."

Julie remembered that her father was extremely depressed that December.

"It would be our second Christmas in the cold and drafty old farmhouse," she said. "And, of course, worst of all, it would be our first Christmas without Mama."

Julie was quick to point out that the family used to have really wonderful Christmases. "We were never rich, but we were well enough off until the Depression wiped Daddy out. But more than our nice home on the family farm, the presents around the Christmas tree, and the delicious holiday dinners, we missed Mama."

Because of the terrible melancholy that had envel-oped their father, Julie did not wish to concern him with her illness, so as much as possible, she suffered in silence.

"One entire day while the other kids were at school, I lay and prayed that we could have more blankets and just a little extra money so that we could have a nicer Christmas and so Daddy would not have to work so hard," she said.

On the afternoon of the Christmas miracle, Julie remembered that she had been huddled next to the oil burner, waiting for the kids to come home from school.

"I knew my fever was getting higher," she said. "I wanted Merrie there with me. She was the oldest, and she always seemed to know that to do. She was like another mom to us younger kids."

Julie heard the front door open. "The sound of the door opening really startled me," she said, "because I knew that Steve, the last one out the door that morning, had locked it behind him."

She turned to see a very handsome man walk into the house. "He was fairly tall, well built, and he had long blond hair that reached nearly to his shoulders," she said. "I couldn't think of any man around those parts who wore his hair so long."

Julie started to say something about trespassing, but he just smiled at her. "I will never forget his bright blue eyes," she said. "And the way he lifted one hand as if to indicate that he had come in peace, that he wouldn't hurt me."

The stranger had four thick blankets under one arm, and he set them down on the kitchen table.

For the first time, Julie noticed that he wore hardly anything at all against the cold North Dakota winter weather.

"He had on just a thin white shirt and a pair of blue jeans," Julie said. "I could see that he meant to give us those blankets, so I spoke up and told him, 'You'd better keep a couple of those for yourself, Mister. You'll like to freeze to death in this awful cold.'"

The handsome stranger smiled, and he spoke for the first time. "He spoke in this very unusual, beautiful, rich voice," Julie said. "It was kind of like he was somehow singing and talking at the same time. 'I won't need them, thank you,' he said. 'They are for you.'"

Just before he left, the man took four $20 bills from his shirt pocket and set them on top of the blankets. "A little extra money," he said with a broad smile.

He was almost to the door when he turned to her and said in that same talking/singing voice, "You'll soon be better, Julie. Merry Christmas."

And then he was gone.

"Immediately after he left," Julie said, "I knew that I had just seen an angel. He had come in answer to my prayers. I had asked for some more blankets and 'a little extra money,' and that was just what he had left us."

When Merrie, Steve, and Larry came home from school, Julie told them excitedly that an angel had brought them four new blankets and some money.

"Merrie felt my forehead and said something about how my fever felt so high," Julie said. "She covered me with the new blankets and poured hot tea down my throat until the fever broke."

That night when he came home worn out from work at the elevator, their father listened carefully to Julie's story about the angel who had brought blankets and money. Angel or benevolent neighbor, he knew that the four $20 bills that the man had left would provide just the kind of buffer he needed to catch up on some bills and to be able to provide better for his children.

"Daddy always felt that some nice young man in town or on one of the neighboring farms had learned of our hard times and had taken it upon himself to give us the blankets and the money," Julie said. "Eighty dollars might not seem like much today, but back in those days of depression in the 1930s, it really helped Daddy to start to climb back on his feet."

Julie said that her brothers and older sister always believed that her identification of the stranger as an angel who had heard her prayers for blankets and some money was the correct one. They agreed that there wasn't anyone in town or country or anywhere in the county who resembled their handsome, longhaired benefactor.

"Even then, I was a really good artist," she said, "and I was able to draw a very accurate sketch of the benevolent stranger. We lived in that community for another eight years, and none of us kids ever saw anyone who looked the way he did.

"I will always believe that it was an angel who paid us a visit just before Christmas and helped us to survive that terrible winter. I will believe that until the day I die. And then I know that I will see him again."

*W*e Steigers don't know why we were so surprised when John Fisher told us that he believed in Santa Claus. Perhaps it was because John was fifty-six years old, a graduate of an Ivy League university, and a successful New Hampshire businessman.

John motioned for the waitress to bring a fresh pot of coffee to our booth. "I believe that Santa exists," he said, "because I saw him bring gifts to my sister Ruby and me when I was eight years old."

We were sitting in an all-night restaurant with a man we had known for about five years. We had first met him when he attended one of our lectures in New York City in 1987, and we had become friends through a continued correspondence. He was an intelligent man with a quick wit and a compassionate heart, and he had managed to become extremely successful in his retail business without compromising his strict spiritual ethics.

For years, he had wanted to sponsor us in his hometown, and in 1992, we scheduled a seminar with him for the first weekend in December. It would be our final appearance for the year.

Now, we settled back in the restaurant booth and asked him to tell us about the night that he had seen Santa Claus.

When he was young, John began, his family had been very poor. "Of course, when you're a kid, you really have little concept of whether or not your family is rich or poor," he said. "My father, Stephen Fisher, always managed to have food on the table and made enough as a truck driver to allow us to keep the lights on and the furnace running—although I remember it was always set very low, even during the coldest weather. My mom and Ruby always wore heavy sweaters to keep warm. But when you're three or four, you care very little about social status as long as there is food in your tummy and a roof over your head. It's when you start school that you find out just where you belong on the social pecking order."

Although the onset of the Christmas season always posed a major challenge to Stephen and Alma Fisher, somehow they managed to come up with a few gifts for Santa to place around the tree on Christmas morning.

"I am certain that, compared to the presents that some of the children in better-off families received, our toys would have been considered cheap," John said, "but to Ruby and me, they were wonderful."

When John started school in 1943, World War II had already taken many young fathers from the small town in New Hampshire. Because Stephen Fisher had been born with his right leg considerably shorter than his left, he was not eligible for the draft. "But the fact that so many men had been drafted or had volunteered for the armed forces didn't help Dad find work," John said. "A lot of the storekeepers, wanting to help with the war effort, hired the wives of men who had left home to fight the enemies overseas, thereby contributing to the support of a fighting man's family. There was nothing wrong with this reasoning in principle, but it left Dad with only handy-man type work that paid very little."

In spite of these very difficult times, the Fishers always celebrated Christmas to the fullest extent that their meager budget would allow. And John and his sister would lie in their beds on Christmas Eve, barely able to keep from trembling, as they dreamed about Santa Claus and what he might bring them.

"When I was in first grade, all the kids believed in Santa," John recalled. "We were all true believers who knew that it was Santa Claus who brought all those gifts on Christmas morning. In second grade, the ranks of the believers began to thin, and heretics among us whispered that there was no Santa Claus.

Some insisted on voicing the absurd notion that it was only one's parents who placed those gifts under the tree while the children slept. By third grade, I was one of only a few devout believers who were keeping the faith."

In the summer of 1945, when John was in the third grade, the terrible war ended, and by the holiday season, the stores were filled once again with toys made of metal, rubber, and wood, rather than cardboard, paper, and sawdust. "It was absolutely mind-boggling to walk past the department stores and the dime stores and behold the marvelous array of toys," John said. "I spotted a red fire engine that I wanted so badly that I became dizzy with longing every time I thought of it. Ruby's dolls had always been made of stockings with button eyes, and she had fallen under the spell of a doll that had a realistic ceramic face with bright blue eyes and golden curls that cascaded down over its forehead.

"We wrote out our list to send to Santa at the North Pole; and as convincing as an eight-year-old boy and a five-year-old girl could be, we vowed our belief in the reality of his being and swore that we had been so good that the very angels adored us."

That same afternoon, the angels must have been looking the other way when John got into a fight with his friend Randy Sommers, who had called him a baby for still believing in Santa Claus. Dennis Murray, John's best friend, had to break up the fight and make the two boys shake hands.

"Dennis was an agnostic about Santa," John said. "He still wanted to believe, but I could see in his eyes as we walked home that afternoon that he had doubts."

What John didn't know at that time was that his father had run a red light with his old pickup in his haste to make as many deliveries as possible that day, and the fine levied against him in traffic court had depleted the meager savings that he had set aside to buy Christmas presents. Stephen Fisher had come home that evening, leaned his head on his wife's shoulder, and gave her the sad news. The children would receive no gifts at all that year. How could he face them on Christmas morning?

Alma Fisher wiped the tears from her eyes and told her hard-working, caring husband that they would just have to pray for a miracle that Christmas.

On Christmas Eve, John and Ruby sat quietly on the sofa in front of the Christmas tree.

"We had both noticed that Mom and Dad had acted very strangely during dinner," John said, "and a seed of doubt had entered my mind. I didn't want to spoil things for my little sister, but I had begun to wonder if maybe the kids who teased me about believing in Santa had been right. I began to figure that perhaps the reason that Mom and Dad had been so quiet and kept giving each other weird looks throughout the meal was because they had hidden away all these wonderful toys. They were probably wondering how they were going to get them out of the hiding places and under the tree without our seeing them.

"I decided that I would somehow stay awake that night and see for myself once and for all if Dad and Mom were really the ones who gave us our gifts and if Santa was just a story for little kids."

John recalled how he lay there in the dark after bedtime, listening quietly for any sound that might betray his father or mother getting out of bed and going down the stairs. "It must have been very late when I heard a peculiar kind of humming sound in the living room," he said. "I got out of bed and peered down into the darkness. I gasped out loud when I saw a bright light and a shadowy figure moving around the Christmas tree. I crept down a few more steps, and I saw a really eerie light and shadows literally bouncing around the room. I figured that it had to be Dad with a flashlight."

In the next few moments, John was puzzled when the eerily glowing light seemed to move directly through the wall and exit the house. "I got a glimpse of it outside the living room window before it disappeared," John said. "I thought that somehow Dad must have got outside, but I knew he couldn't stay out there long in his pajamas, for it was really cold. I decided to sit there on the steps until Dad came back inside. I would quietly confront him with my newly gained knowledge of the Santa subterfuge, but I would promise not to spoil things for Ruby."

John sat there for what seemed hours, drawing his bathrobe tight around him to keep warm. "Then I heard Mom and Dad speaking in their bedroom," John said. "Since I was sitting there in the middle of the stairs like a little troll on a bridge, there was no way that either of them could have come up the stairs without passing me. I got up, crossed the hall, and knocked softly on the door to their bedroom."

When he entered, John was astonished to see his father sitting up on the side of the bed, being comforted by his mother. "I had never seen Dad cry before, and I had no idea how to respond," John said. "Then Mom said that Dad was heartbroken because they had no money to buy Ruby and me even the smallest of presents for Christmas. I kind of started to giggle because I thought they were teasing me, keeping up the Santa charade. I had seen someone moving around the Christmas tree in the living room."

Fearing an intruder, his father went to investigate, baseball bat securely in hand. When he clicked on the lights, he gasped in amazement and shouted for everyone to come downstairs. There around the tree was the red fire engine that John had wanted so badly. And next to it was Ruby's doll with the golden curls. And there were other gifts, including some for Mom and Dad.

"In spite of my parents' protests to the contrary,

I assumed that they had pulled off an major illusion on behalf of the Santa myth," John said. "But as the days went by with Dad and Mom insisting that they had nothing to do with the gifts, I began to believe that some kind of Christmas miracle had occurred in our humble home."

John's parents believed that Uncle Don and Aunt Jan, who were aware of their financial problems, had crept in with a flashlight and left the gifts so the children wouldn't be disappointed at Christmas. They also suggested their next door neighbors, the Murrays, as possible candidates who might have done such a good deed.

"But for years to come, Uncle Don, Aunt Jan, and the Murrays next door always denied that they had anything to do with it," John said, concluding his story. "So if Mom and Dad, my aunt and uncle, and the Murrays next door had nothing to do with our Christmas miracle, that's why I believe in Santa Claus. The skeptics can stay with the benevolent neighbors or relatives theory, but I long ago understood that what I saw that night was a holy light moving around next to the

Christmas tree. I saw the very spirit of Santa Claus and the very energy of unconditional love manifesting to fulfill two little kids' dreams of a merry Christmas."

*E*ver since he was a little boy, Rick Horton's favorite holiday had always been Christmas, and he gloried in every aspect of the season. Nothing could keep Rick from a joyful celebration of Christmas.

Then, on December 4, 1987, a sudden heart attack at the age of thirty-eight took him from his wife, Melba, his three young children, and his loving parents, Louise and Charles.

In spite of the heavy cloud of grief that hung over the family, his parents decided that they would do everything that they could to make the Christmas holiday season as happy as possible. They knew that Rick would have wanted it that way.

Louise and Charles set about decorating their house, inside and out, just as they had since Rick was a small boy. They made certain that Melba and the grandkids knew that they were to come for a big turkey dinner on Christmas Eve and that they would all go to church as a family on Christmas Day. Everything would be just as it would have been if Rick had not died—for they knew that he was very much with them in spirit.

As Louise and Charles were assembling the miniature manger scene that they had placed on the fireplace mantel ever since Rick was seven, it came to them that they should fashion a small home altar to commemorate the memory of their son. They bought a terrarium to honor Rick's love of plants and nature, and Charles filled a tall purple urn with scented water. Around Rick's picture, they placed a tall red candle in a bright green holder and a number of Christmas-tree ornaments to add the touch of holiday color that he had always loved so much. Just off to the left, they placed a small incense burner in which they burned cones of sandalwood three or four times a day.

Solemnly, just a few days before Christmas, Charles lighted the tall red candle, and Louise placed a Bible on the altar and opened it to the story of the first Christmas as recorded in the Gospel of Matthew. Both of them gave silent prayers toward the same unspoken request: that they be given some sign that Rick's spirit was a happy one.

Louise began to cry softly, then lowered her head against her husband's shoulder.

"Don't cry, Mom," he comforted her, taking one of her hands in his own. "If there is any way between Heaven and earth for Rick to make contact with us, you know that he will find it."

Louise smiled. Charles had tried to tame their son's assertive personality when he was a boy, but he had come to admire Rick's aggressiveness. Their Rick had the knack of knowing how to turn on the charm and push for what he truly believed in, and he had used this talent well through high school, college, and the business world. If only he hadn't been taken from his family when he was so young, when he was just beginning to achieve a high level of personal and professional success.

Brushing back a tear, Charles chuckled softly. "You know, there didn't seem to be anything that Rick couldn't figure out," he said. "Rick had that stubborn streak that made him just keep at things until he was satisfied he knew what they were all about. If there is a way to bring us a message, you know he will."

On Christmas Eve day, Louise was up early to begin preparing a hearty meal for the family. In her mind, she had carefully planned the events of Christmas for the Horton family: Melba and the children would arrive about five o'clock for an early dinner. When they had finished eating, everyone would help clean up and then it would be time to open the presents under the Christmas tree. After the excitement of watching the kids unwrap their gifts, they would all enjoy some tasty glasses of eggnog—with a little something special added for the grown-ups. Then Melba and the grandkids would stay overnight so they could all attend an early church service the next morning.

Louise was somewhat annoyed when Melba and the grandkids burst into the house an hour earlier than she had mentally scheduled their arrival. Louise knew that she could be an awful perfectionist fussbudget about such matters—especially when she had everything worked out in her own mind—but she found herself getting a bit nervous and irritated when she felt as though the evening would not proceed as smoothly as she had visualized. She knew that the grandkids would start snooping around the presents and getting into things they shouldn't. Charles was sitting in the living room reading the evening paper, so she knew he wouldn't be doing much policing of his grandchildren. Melba asked if she could help, but Louise was fussy about finishing things that she had started.

Although she loved Christmas carols as much as anyone, Louise found the music coming from the radio getting on her nerves. Under any other circumstances, she would have enjoyed the familiar holiday melodies, but because of the stress of checking the turkey in the oven, preparing the trimmings for a perfect dinner, keeping an eye on the gifts under the tree, and feeling the pressure of guests—even if they were family—who had arrived an hour early, Louise found herself shouting at her husband: "Charlie, I know it's Christmas Eve, but can we please do without the carols for a little while?"

Charles was puzzled. "I beg your pardon, Mom. What did you say?"

With her nerves frazzled, Louise took his question to signal resistance to her subtle request to shut off the radio. She raised her voice, trying her very best not to sound really nasty: "Please, at least until I finish preparing dinner, please shut off the radio."

Charles stood in the kitchen doorway. "Mom, there's no radio, no television, no phonograph playing Christmas music anywhere in this house," he said quietly.

And then, for the first time, they all began to pay attention to the music that was filtering through the house. It was a lovely, haunting melody, strangely familiar, yet none of them could identify it. Sometimes there would be a chorus of voices with the music; other times, there would be only the lovely orchestral sounds filling the air around them.

"It definitely has a Christmas flavor to it," Melba said. "But it is no hymn or popular holiday song that I know."

Louise, Charles, Melba, and the three children looked everywhere for the source of the beautiful melody. Charles even went outside to see if someone had left a radio or tape player going in a car parked somewhere in the street. But search as they might— downstairs, upstairs, in the basement and attic—they could not locate the source of the wonderful music.

And then they all began to move to the one place that they had, on one level of awareness, been avoiding.

"We began to move toward the altar that Charles and I had prepared to commemorate Rick's passing," Louise said.

Melba began to weep as the entire family, including the children, heard the ethereal, angelic music coming from the Christmas ornaments arranged around Rick's photographs.

"It was a true Christmas miracle," Louise said. "It was as if each of the ornaments was some kind of receiving set for the beautiful, unearthly music that was being broadcast from Heaven."

"Rick always loved Christmas music," Charles said, his eyes misting with tears. "And now he's somehow arranged to send some very special Christmas music to us from the angels on high."

And then, just as suddenly as the music had begun, it stopped.

Louise suddenly had a clear mental image of what was occurring on that most remarkable Christmas Eve.

"The radio," she said. "Rick wants us to turn on the radio. While I was fussing that I wanted a radio off, Rick was trying to get us to turn the radio on."

Charles clicked on the old console model they still kept in the living room. The very first sounds that flowed from the radio were the words from the poignant holiday song that promises that the singer will be home for Christmas.

"We all stood there, tears flowing freely," Louise said. "We all hugged each other, and those of us who knew the words sang along with the radio. We all felt Rick right there in the midst of us, hugging us, and singing along."

Charles smiled, his voice quavering as he spoke: "I told you Rick would find a way to let us know that he was all right. He did it. Rick came home for Christmas."

Louise concluded by saying that she believes that her son gave his family the greatest Christmas gift possible. "His spirit demonstrated the truth of the Christmas promise. He gave his children a proof of life everlasting that will strengthen them all the days of their lives."

*W*henever seventy-three-year-old Lanette Willert tells the story of her Christmas miracle, her voice grows soft and you can see tears begin to well up in the corners of her eyes; for even though it took place many years ago, the memory of that long-ago Christmas remains as fresh in her mind as if it had occurred only yesterday.

When she was a young girl, Lanette's family lived in a small town in Minnesota, far enough north where they seldom had to worry whether or not they would have a white Christmas. She was Lanette Petersen then, and she remembers December 1943 as seeming particularly cold and beset with one blizzard after another.

"I was sixteen that winter and considered myself quite a grown lady," Lanette said. "Because so many of our hometown boys had enlisted to fight the Nazis and the Japanese in the war, I read the paper and listened to the news on the radio so I could take part in conversations with the adults who gathered to discuss current events at the soda fountain and the restaurant. And I never missed going to church every Sunday to pray for all the GIs—and especially our hometown boys—and ask God that they come home safely. Since Christmas was just around the corner, the church was going to have a couple of special programs to remind everyone of the true spirit of Christmas, which was to bring peace to Earth."

Lanette's little brother, Karl, was going to play a piano solo at the Sunday school program. "We were so proud of Karl," she said. "He was only ten years old, but he could really play the piano. He had started lessons when he was seven, and by the time he was eight, folks in town were calling him a little genius. He had played solos at several school band concerts and even a couple of times with the adults at the summer concerts in the park. At the Christmas Sunday school program that December, Karl would first play 'Away in a Manger' as a solo, then the third and fourth graders would assemble around the piano and Karl would accompany their singing of the carol. Of course, being Lutherans, we knew that Martin Luther had written 'Away in a Manger,' so this really had special meaning to us."

Every night Karl would practice, perfecting his talent, improving his skill. In those days, families provided most of their own entertainment in the evenings, and

the Petersen family had little Karl on the keys to sup-
plement the radio or phonograph.

"Dad and Mom—Virgil and Dorothy Petersen—
would usually read books or magazines in the evenings,
and sometimes, after homework, I would listen to some
news or comedy shows on the radio," Lanette said, "but
Karl provided excellent background music for whatever
the family was doing."

For many years afterward, Lanette blamed herself
for what occurred late one afternoon as she was walking home from her part-time job at the soda fountain.

"Karl had hung around the store waiting to walk
home with me," she said. "Although Mr. Monson had
a sign tacked to the magazine rack that warned, 'This
isn't the public library. No free reading,' I would let
Karl read some comic books if he stayed out of sight in
a back booth."

Lanette remembered that it was several degrees
below zero and it was already dark when her boyfriend,
Robert, suddenly appeared beside them and asked her
to go sledding on Martinson's Hill. Lanette replied
with great resolve and told him that she was due at
home for supper—and besides, she couldn't let Karl
walk home alone after he had waited so long for her at
the soda fountain.

"Robert was really convincing," Lanette said, "arguing that just a couple of runs down the hill wouldn't

take that long. And he played up to Karl, saying that he just knew that my little brother would love to go sledding with the big kids."

Karl was excited by the prospect of joining a group of teenagers on their bobsleds on Martinson's Hill. "We just called them bobsleds," Lanette said. "They were just big sleds that two or three of us kids could sit on at the same time. Martinson's Hill had the advantage of a long slope that seemed to go on forever, and it was fun sledding with the gang. And the fact that it was after dark made it seem all the more exciting."

Lanette insisted that they would join Robert for only a couple of runs down the hill, and the three of them set out for Martinson's Hill on the edge of town.

"I will never forget how the wind seemed to slice right through my parka," Lanette said. "It was crazy to go sledding when it was so cold, but we were Scandinavian-Americans from Minnesota who were supposed to have fun in freezing temperatures, just as our Viking ancestors had romped about on the ice floes above the Arctic Circle."

Lanette kept a scarf over her mouth and nose so that she could breathe without the wind blowing frigid air down her throat, but Karl had neither a scarf nor a parka.

"He had a heavy wool coat and a stocking cap that he pulled down over his ears," she said. "He seemed to be having so much fun, and he wasn't complaining about being cold—so we probably took five or six runs down the hill. But when we finally decided that we had better get home for supper, Karl was shivering. We still had quite a ways to walk from the sledding hill to our home, so his lips seemed almost blue with cold before we walked in the front door."

Two or three nights later, when Karl was practicing his solo for the Christmas pageant, Lanette heard him stop playing to put a hand to his chest and release a series of hoarse, barking coughs.

"Mom was instantly alert to the sounds of any colds or sickness in the Petersen household," Lanette recalled, "so she advised Karl that she would be rubbing his chest with Vicks when he went to bed. Dad set aside his news-paper and asked Karl if he was feeling okay."

Karl nodded and continued playing "Away in a Manger." He admitted that he had a sore throat and a tickle that made him cough. That night, the family was kept awake by the ten-year-old's rasping cough. The next morning, Dorothy insisted that he be taken to Dr. Wayne to have him see to that ugly cough.

"I'm feeling better, Mom," Karl protested. "I'll pick up some cough drops on the way to school."

Seemingly pacified by Karl's apparent improve-ment, Dorothy let him go to school, but a bleary-eyed Virgil announced in a grumpy tone that he would also pick up some cough medicine at the drugstore so they could all get some sleep that night.

After supper that evening, as Karl was practicing the piano, he began coughing and pressed a hand to his chest. "Mom, I have such a terrible pain here."

Lanette watched her mother rush to Karl and feel his forehead. "Virgil, this boy is burning with fever," she said, her face drawn and anxious. "Call Dr. Wayne."

Those were the days when doctors made house calls—but those were also the days before modern miracle drugs and antibiotics.

Lanette recalled listening outside Karl's bedroom door as Dr. Wayne examined her brother. She will always remember her mother's cry of fear when the doctor cautiously diagnosed pneumonia.

Dr. Wayne did his best to sustain a mother's hope: "Now, Dorothy, the fever, the chills, the sharp pain in the chest indicate pneumonia, but let's be strong and not give in to anxiety. We'll just work hard with Karl and break that congestion right out of him. After all, we can't disappoint his audience at the Sunday school program, can we?"

"For ten days and nights, we all did whatever we could to help Karl get better," Lanette said. "Karl kept saying over and over how he would get well, how he would play 'Away in a Manger' for the pageant. But he insisted that I help him walk downstairs to practice.

The Sunday school program was only a few days away. It just broke my heart to have to tell him that he had to stay in bed."

Once, Lanette recalled, she entered Karl's room to find him moving his fingers on the bed covers as if he were playing the piano. He explained that he could "play" the stripes on the blankets as if they were piano keys.

And then Karl took a sad and pronounced turn for the worst, and he could only lie still in bed, trembling with fever, fighting for every breath of air that he could force into his lungs.

On a cold and awful winter's night just six days before Christmas, Dr. Wayne slowly moved the blankets over Karl's silent face and body. Through Lanette's grief and guilt, she heard the doctor say something about "edema in the lungs" having quieted forever her brother's talent and spirit.

A few nights after the funeral, the Petersen family was seated in the front room at the table, trying their best to appreciate the chicken dinner that Grandmother Sorenson had brought over for their family meal.

"I saw Mom look over at the Christmas tree," Lanette said, "and she began to cry when she saw the gaily wrapped presents that Karl would never open. I guess that's when I remembered that it was Christmas Eve and I felt sad that that holiest of nights would never again be the same for any of us."

Grandma Sorenson managed to get the family around the table, urging them to eat some dinner and try to bring something of the Christmas spirit into their hearts. She had just asked the blessing for the meal when they all heard the first notes come from the piano.

"We were all startled, and we all turned in our chairs to look at the keyboard," Lanette said. "I remember that I felt a shiver run up my spine. Then once again the keys sounded—and we all recognized the opening notes of 'Away in a Manger.' We all heard it as clearly as if Karl were sitting there in front of us, playing the piano."

Virgil Petersen reached out to take his wife's hand firmly in his own. "It's Karl," he said softly, tears moving over his cheeks. "It sounds just as he would play it."

Dorothy lowered her head, not daring to believe. "Is . . . is it possible?"

Once again, the notes sounded from the piano, and Lanette whispered the words of the familiar Christmas hymn: "Away in a manger, no crib for his bed, the little Lord Jesus lay down his sweet head. . . ."

Grandmother Sorenson nodded solemnly. "Our Lord promises that we will all be joined together once again in heaven. The angels are giving us a sign right now, letting our little Karl come to play the piano for us one last time."

"Can it really be Karl?" Dorothy cried out from the depth of her mother's heart.

The notes sounded louder than before, then, once again, very faintly. "Thank the blessed Lord," Lanette heard her mother say, "our little Karl is now playing for the angels in Heaven."

Lanette concluded her Christmas miracle story by saying that after that special Christmas Eve, they never again heard any heavenly notes sounding from the old upright piano. "Even though God had taken our beloved brother at Christmastime, he also granted us all the greatest Christmas gift of all—proof of the survival of the spirit after death. We were all able to lead more spiritual lives after that Christmas Eve because of our certainty that the soul lives on."

*S*usan Klemp was half asleep when she thought she heard her infant daughter crying. She opened her eyes, looked about the room, and was startled to see that the bed lamp had been turned on and a man was leaning over the cradle.

"My God!" she gasped. Her brain struggled with a hundred different fears.

Her husband, Gus, was on a three-day ice fishing trip with friends. She was alone.

Did the intruder mean to injure little Gretchen?

Why had she let Gus go on that silly trip so close to Christmas? All right, so he was a high school sociology teacher and those few days during Christmas vacation gave him his only chance to indulge in his favorite hobby—but it was only three days until Christmas Eve!

And now there was a burglar in the house.

Then she heard the man singing softly to the infant, "Silent Night," in German, just as Gus liked to do, the way his grandmother had taught him when he was a boy.

Susan got out of bed, forgetting for the moment that she should either be calling the police or getting Gus's revolver out of its hiding place in a dresser drawer.

"Who are you?" she asked the man. He had drawn the hood of his heavy coat over his face so she couldn't distinguish any of his features in the dim light.

"Who are you?" she repeated, trying her best to dismiss all inflections of fear from her voice.

The man raised his head, and Susan was shocked to recognize her husband.

"Oh, Gus, you big lug, why did you come home without telling me?" she asked, tears of relief clouding her eyes.

Susan collapsed on the edge of the bed, nervous laughter releasing her pent-up tensions. "Do you know that you nearly scared the life out of me?" she scolded.

Then she noticed that his coat was soaked and that it was dripping water that smelled strongly of fish and Canadian lake.

"Don't get Gretchen wet with your stinky fish water!" she said sharply. "How did you get so wet?"

Susan walked into the bathroom and got Gus a thick towel.

"You get those wet things off," she told him, "while I go make you some hot coffee. I'm so glad you're home in plenty of time for us to get some last-minute Christmas presents for your brother's family."

As Susan was putting on her robe, she heard Gus once again humming "Silent Night" over Gretchen's cradle. She was just leaving the room when the bed lamp went out.

Susan called for Gus to turn the light back on, but he didn't answer. She fumbled for the light switch for the ceiling light, found it at last, and turned it on.

Gus was gone.

Susan never saw him again.

On the same night that his image had stood over their infant daughter's cradle, singing a Christmas hymn, he had broken through the ice in a faraway Canadian lake. Gus Klemp's body was never recovered, but his spirit had come home to say farewell and to share a Christmas miracle with his wife and baby daughter.

*D*aniel Gomez felt his heart sink to his knees. How could this have happened again, and so close to Christmas? For the third time in six years, he was laid off his job, only this time it looked like the company was going to be permanently out of business.

Each time before, he and several other employees were promised an increase in pay and benefits as soon as the company could reorganize and restructure things. Although it often took longer than expected, each time they called Daniel back to work, his boss reassured him that the problems were being worked out. Since the commitments of a slight increase in salary and a few extra "perks" had been honored, Daniel had no reason to doubt the current solidity of his employer. Things had been going very well for the last several years, with no hint of the impending calamity, when this, the final notification—the dreaded pink slip—came. The timing couldn't have been worse. His wife, Sarah, was pregnant with their third child, and not in good health. For several weeks, she had been experiencing tightness in her chest and was having a difficult time breathing, but she insisted she was probably just suffering from allergies or a winter cold that would soon pass. She refused to go to the doctor, not wanting to add any more bills to their already overstretched budget. With two other children, one seven years old and one four, there never seemed to be an extra dollar left after their monthly expenses were met. But now, when Daniel arrived home, he knew there was no choice but to take Sarah to the doctor—no matter how much she protested.

The second he kissed Sarah hello, Daniel knew that she had a fever and had taken a turn for the worse. There was now an audible wheezing in her chest, so without saying another word, he went to the phone, called the doctor, rounded up seven-year-old Katie and little Jonathan, then returned to the bedroom with a pile of winter snowsuits, coats, hats, boots, and mittens, which he dumped on the floor. As he started to sort out whose coat belonged to whom—he announced to his wife that Dr. Zachariah was waiting for her and he wouldn't take no for an answer. He decided it best not to mention anything about their current employment status, fearing the stress of the news would further aggravate her condition.

It took every ounce of energy Daniel could muster up from deep within him to entertain the children with a positive spirit and remain hopeful while their mama was in the examination room with the doctor. Unfortunately, little Jonathan brought up Santa Claus and what he wanted for Christmas, which was now only three and a half weeks away. Daniel suddenly felt a growing tightness in his own chest as the mere mention of Santa reminded him that he was without a job, so there might not be a Santa this year. Then, as he glanced up, he noticed the doctor approaching with a not-so-pleasant look on his face. Noticing the presence of the children, Dr. Zachariah turned to the reception desk and requested several lollipops and some assistance to watch over the kids while he talked with Mr. Gomez.

"How is she, Doctor . . . do you know anything yet?" Daniel blurted out.

Sensing Daniel's anxiety, Dr. Zachariah tried to tone down the seriousness of Sarah's condition, yet emphasize the importance of medical attention. "Your wife told me you have been trying to get her to come in for the last several weeks, and that she refused, thinking she would be fine. But," he continued, "I can tell you this, if you had not insisted in bringing her now—even another twelve hours might have been too late. She is down getting X rays that I think will confirm my suspicions of pneumonia. It won't be much longer before we know."

The doctor barely finished speaking when he spotted an attendant pushing a wheel chair with Sarah holding an envelope with the X rays on her lap. At that very second, a page calling for Dr. Zachariah was the X ray technician who was relaying his findings to the doctor. It seemed that everything was happening at once. Dr. Zachariah made a motion with his hand that signaled Sarah's being wheeled directly back into the examination room, while he maintained the other arm around Daniel, guiding him to follow along.

Putting the X rays up on the light box, he proclaimed, "Yes, sorry young lady, it will be the hospital for you," he semiscolded, but tempered his words with a wink, adding, "it's a good thing your husband loves you and saw to it to get you in here—in the knick of time. And now we have no time to waste in getting you checked in and started on treatment—immediately! You don't mess around with pneumonia, and it is most definitely what you have." Daniel squeezed Sarah's hand affectionately, kissed it, then attempted to lighten up the moment by teasing her, saying, "See, what did I tell you? You should listen to your hubby!"

With tears in his eyes, he did all he could to hide his desperation. In a moment of near panic, he felt his throat clamp as he swallowed the huge lump that seemed to be welling up from the pit of boiling worries in his stomach, as he realized he didn't even know if they had hospital coverage now—and Sarah didn't even know the other bad news of the day. Still, he managed to assure his wife that the children would be fine and not to worry, the most important thing now was for her to get well.

After the hospital admissions process was started on Sarah, the doctor explained more of the unpleasant details to Daniel. Such a huge percentage of Sarah's lungs was filled with fluid that he was concerned that the baby was not getting enough oxygen. This could mean there was a danger to the life of the unborn baby—as well as to Sarah. Confirming the term of Sarah's pregnancy, Dr. Zachariah added, "We'll do the best we can, now try not to worry too much, and get some rest yourself. You look like you could use some rest, too."

Daniel never remembered a time in his life when he felt such despair. He could barely stammer out the confession to Dr. Zachariah of the other bad news he had received earlier that day. He explained his uncertainty of the insurance coverage as he pleaded that it would not be a factor in getting the best care for his wife and baby.

As compassionate as he could be, Dr. Zachariah pledged that Sarah would be in the finest of care—no matter what the insurance status. "I so hate to bring this up, but no matter how unpleasant, I think it would be advisable that you have a serious talk with your children. As I said before and emphasize again, Sarah

is in grave condition and the children need to understand why she isn't coming home now . . . and even be
prepared if. . . ."

The doctor found it unnecessary to say the rest of
the words, as Daniel's tear-stained face reflected the
anguish of the worst-case scenario as a potential reality.

Daniel took the children home after explaining as
best he could about their mother. As he tucked them
into bed after they were bathed and had eaten an evening snack, he said prayers with them, and then they
all prayed a very special prayer for their mama.

"Daddy, I know God will help mama get better. I
know it, because he told me so when I was saying a prayer
at the hospital," little Jonathan blurted out with complete confidence, as he hugged his daddy goodnight.

"Don't worry, Daddy, she will get all better and be
home for Christmas," he said again, as Daniel turned
off the lights and clicked on the night-light.

Early in the morning, Daniel called the priest at their
church. The whole family was very active in St. Mary's
Parish, and had been for most of the years they had lived
in the Chicago area. He could not keep himself from crying over the phone as he told Father Cassidy about Sarah
and also of being laid off permanently from work.

"Please, Father, will you put Sarah on the prayer
list and do you have time to go see her in the hospital?"
Daniel pleaded.

Father Cassidy prayed with Daniel over the telephone and said he would come to the house right after he visited Sarah in the hospital.

Daniel had already called the hospital to check on Sarah's condition and was attempting to locate a baby-sitter to be with the children while he went to see her. By the time the priest arrived at the house, Daniel had not found anyone, so he was just going to take the children with him and stay as long as he could while they waited in the reception area.

Father Cassidy was very calming and just his presence in the house gave Daniel the courage to face his fears with faith. Telling the priest that he thought he would take the children with him as he was rounding up some books and toys that might occupy them at the hospital, Daniel thanked him profusely for his time and prayers.

Father Cassidy responded by saying there were "things in the works" and soon there might be some more helpful things rounded up as well . . . from the parish. "By tomorrow, I think the good Lord and the good people of St. Mary's will be able to help the Gomez family out just a bit," the father added with a twinkle in his eye and love in his heart.

For nearly two weeks, Sarah remained in very serious condition. She was on a respirator and powerful antibiotics. From all indications, the baby—if it made it—could be brain damaged from the lack of oxygen. The priest had arranged for several ladies of the church to come help with the Gomez children and with chores such as cooking and cleaning, to free Daniel up to be at Sarah's side. The prayer groups at the church were all praying for Sarah and family, even putting them on an international prayer list with a special request for prayer of the pope.

Father Cassidy conducted a special anointing ceremony at Sarah's hospital bedside. A group of dedicated people through the church decided it was important to do a more intensive prayer vigil, and they maintained a "prayer chain" with a volunteer taking an hour at a time, until all twenty-four hours of each and every day were covered with healing and prayer for Sarah, Daniel, and the children. Although there was little or no change in Sarah's health, or that of the unborn baby, during the two weeks, many other miracles began occurring.

Literally, Daniel had gone through what little savings and money he had to buy groceries and pay the bills for that immediate period . . . leaving no money from that point on for any necessities. They were down to the last bar of soap, the cupboards were growing quite bare, and there was not even laundry soap left to wash clothes with. The volunteers grew in number, and many people brought food already prepared in casserole dishes, cookies, and snacks. As the word spread that the shelves in the Gomez family home were about empty, bags of groceries would appear on the doorstep, with nothing but an anonymous note and the ringing of the doorbell to indicate something was there. Money was received in the mail, some checks, some cash—and some anonymous.

This overflow of love and generosity deeply touched Daniel's spirit. He found the weight of the burdens he was carrying get lighter and lighter, until he felt more strength and courage than he ever thought he could have in a whole lifetime. His trust and belief that whatever God had in store for him and for his family would ultimately be for the best to make them stronger, grew.

Faithfully, Daniel spent every moment possible at his wife's side in the hospital. One day, as he went home to shower, grab a bite to eat, and kiss the children, he was greeted by a huge surprise when he returned to the hospital.

He had been gone for only two hours—two hours that showered healing on his beloved wife! Sarah's fever broke like magic, and there she was, sitting up in bed, slightly complaining about how hungry she was and questioning why she was in the hospital.

The entire two, almost three, weeks seemed not to have even occurred. She didn't even know she had been sick! The doctors, nurses, friends, family, and

Father Cassidy were all claiming her sudden healing was absolutely nothing short of a miracle.

Several days later, Sarah was discharged from the hospital, returning to her very ecstatic children and husband. It was still not certain what the outcome would be for the unborn child, but all were hopeful. When first arriving home, Sarah was so amazed that the house was spotless and things were in order that she could hardly contain her excitement. There were more groceries in the pantry and refrigerator than she had ever seen, the children had not even a single toy out of place and had clean clothes in their drawers, there were no piles of dirty clothes in the laundry room, and there were even fresh towels in the bathroom! "How could you possibly do all this while you were working?" she asked in amazement. "I can hardly believe my eyes! Did you get a raise and an early Christmas bonus?

"Oh, shopping for Christmas presents is going to be so much fun! I almost feel good enough to go out right now so we can pick out a real tree and get some more lights so we can decorate inside and out!" Sarah gleefully said, not giving Daniel a chance to respond.

Then suddenly she realized he wasn't responding. Looking into his eyes she could tell something wasn't right.

"Oh, did I spoil the surprise? Wasn't I supposed to know about the raise and the Christmas bonus yet? I'm sorry, sweetie, I am just so happy!" she said while hugging him with a near smothering grip.

Daniel didn't have the heart to tell her. He rationalized that it was more important to keep her in good spirits—which he believed to be an immune-boosting strategy. He would at least give her a few days to get stronger and then he would tell her. Now, he just had to pray the kids didn't say something first. He knew if he told the kids not to . . . that's just when they would slip and say something. He managed to give her a strong hug back and a broad enough smile—along with a twinkle in his eye and a wink that seemed to avert any further questions—and said nothing more, at least, not immediately.

"Oh Mommy, I told Daddy not to worry, that God told me you would get all better. I am sooo happy you are home for Christmas!" Jonathan squealed as he went to hug her around the waist, stopping when he remembered how big she was with child. Then he gently kissed her tummy and said, "I'm happy you are here too, little brother or sister."

Sarah acknowledged his joy while patting him on the head and rubbing his back, then suddenly grabbing his hand and putting it on her tummy. "See, he or she heard you, Jonathan. The baby is kicking, feel."

Sarah turned to Daniel and said, "I really think everything is going to be just wonderful. The baby seems fine!"

Katie's motherly instinct had her fluffing up the pillows as she had just retrieved a blanket and was making a cozy place for Mom to sit on the couch in front of the television. "Can I feel too, Mom?" she gingerly asked, feeling like she might be too big for such things. "Of course, darling, let me just sit down in the perfect little place you have readied for me, and I think you will feel the baby still kicking," Sarah said as she stroked Katie's long pony tail that was topped by a big, fancy red-lace bow. "My, don't you look pretty, Katie! Did you wash and brush your hair all by yourself?"

Daniel balked. "Ummm, well, we had a little help. . . ." he began to stutter, as Sarah quickly caught on and coyly smiled her unspoken acknowledgment that help was okay, too. Daniel held his breath and hoped that the kids wouldn't pick up on that and spill the real extent of it. They didn't. The baby kicking again saved the day, as that became the talk of the eve until bedtime. Katie and Jonathan were guessing and bantering back and forth if it was going to be a girl or a boy and what they wanted as names for either. Sarah and Daniel made the decision to not find out the gender, but looked forward to the surprise.

Soon it was time to tuck the kids into bed, say prayers with them, and then get ready for bed themselves. Both husband and wife decided that it would be wise to go to bed early, as they were both exhausted and the reality about how long Sarah had been gone had finally sunk in.

Daniel was up early the next day, and had the table set for breakfast with pancakes, freshly made and keeping warm in the oven. The smell of hot coffee and sausage and bacon sizzling on the stove, awakened the rest of the family in a hurry.

As Sarah shuffled out to kitchen with her wooly slippers dragging and wrapped in her thick winter robe, she kissed her husband good morning, and said, "Wow, how long do I get to be pampered like this? Did they give you the week off, too?"

Daniel kissed her back as he motioned for her to go ahead and sit down, while he pulled out her chair and asked Katie to pour the orange juice.

Feeling very guilty that all the insinuations were bordering now on lies, he didn't think he was going to be able to wait to tell her the truth. Christmas was only four more days away, and he knew she would want to go right out and do shopping and decorating—even though she realized she was supposed to be taking it easy.

"Honey, there is something I really need to talk with you about," he murmured in a low voice, feeling that all-too-familiar queasy feeling in his stomach again.

Once again, he was saved by a child, this time it wasn't the unborn child's kicks, but little Jonathan knocking over his glass of orange juice. Juice ran all over the table, onto Katie, and spilled down onto Mom's robe. The panic of the cold juice everywhere interrupted the continuing glum thoughts in Daniel's head, and he was most grateful. Something he never thought would happen. He was actually happy that one of the kids had spilled something at the table! He knew he would have to face the truth-telling soon, but for now . . . saved by the mess!

Many hours later, when all were dressed and settled into the newness and excitement of Mom being home and Christmas around the corner, Santa's impending visit was brought up.

"Well, ah . . . Sarah, I really do have some things I have to say to you, and I guess I'd better do it now," Daniel said.

Sensing it wasn't good news by the look on her husband's face, Sarah suggested to Katie that she take Jonathan and go watch television for a little bit while she and Daddy talked—then they would go shopping. Katie took Jonathan by the hand and went into the family room, wanting to please her Mother.

Daniel said a silent prayer as he sat Sarah down on the couch, cushioning her back against several pillows, which he fluffed to support her head and neck. Then, taking her legs, he stretched them out, seated himself at the edge of the couch, and started to remove a slipper and give her a foot rub. "Ooooh, that is just what I need." Sarah groaned with pleasure.

The words came more easily to Daniel after he prayed. It was as though the faith that pulled him through the whole ordeal was stronger than ever now, and he believed that God would give Sarah the strength as well, to face their uncertain future together. At least they had each other, their health back, and two wonderful children and all indications of a third coming soon.

Tears streamed down Sarah's cheeks as Daniel told her the scenario as it unfolded from the beginning; about his job loss, sense of despair, turning to Father Cassidy, and then the miracles that came from God through the church. He told of all the help and gifts they had received, from food to groceries left on the steps to money in the mail to volunteers too numerous to mention, who babysat, cleaned, cooked, and did the laundry.

"I didn't want you to worry and I knew you would, so I thought it would be best not to say anything at all until you were stronger, but . . . well, I just don't feel right with you thinking the opposite . . . a raise, Christmas bonus, and all," he said.

Sarah wiggled her toes out from under Daniel's loving massage and reached over to give him a hug. "Oh, you poor darling," she said softly as tears continued to flow.

No more words were spoken as they remained in the embrace for what seemed an eternity—until the baby kicked and they both laughed out loud.

At that moment the phone rang. Daniel got up to answer it, as the phone was in the other room.

When he returned to the living room, his ear-to-ear smile revealed the call to have been a good one. It was Father Cassidy asking Daniel's permission to give his phone number to a parishioner fairly new to the church. The man had called Father Cassidy because he had heard that Mr. Gomez was highly skilled in a particular area, and he was looking for someone to manage a division of the company he was transferred to the area to oversee. Later that day, more was learned about the potential job, but the interview would not be until the first of the New Year.

The Divine love and mercy they had received through Sarah's miracle healing, and the overflow of love and generosity of the church, overwhelmingly touched them both—at the same instant—as they sat together holding hands. Daniel explained the phone conversation regarding the possible future employment to Sarah. "God has truly blessed us with so much," he said, "let's give a prayer of thanks."

Bowing their heads and still holding hands, they each prayed out loud, then hugged and cried again.

"Surely there are no gifts greater than those we have already received that we could have for Christmas," Sarah said. "But what will we do about gifts for the children?"

"Don't worry about us," Katie shouted, betraying her peeking and listening from just around the corner. "We'll be okay, Mama, we'll still have presents under the tree, you'll see!"

Katie's words were barely out when Jonathan beat her to the couch. "Yeah, you'll see," he added, not really knowing with certainty what was meant by that.

"Come on, kids," Daniel blurted out with an exultant tone in his voice, indicating his inner feeling that things truly would be okay, and happy for the way his family was responding to this crisis now nearly passed. "Come sit down by Mommy and Daddy. Let's have a little family talk," he said as he scooted over, making room on the couch.

He then proceeded to explain the situation in more detail, as much as he felt they were capable of understanding, as Sarah chimed in now and then with an affirmative "We'll get by with God's help."

After another group hug, Katie took Jonathan by the hand as she told Mom and Dad they had some secret things to do for Christmas. Off they went, asking to have, "No peeking."

To this, Daniel and Sarah laughed with the sense that they had done all right so far in raising their kids, if they could be that loving when they were just told there wasn't any money for Christmas gifts. Maybe, though, just maybe, there might be a little after Christmas.

Sarah resisted her motherly concern and instinct to check in on what the kids were up to as she could hear things falling in first one room and then in another, and she knew they were going from room to room and even to the garage, rummaging and getting into who knew what kind of mischief. Knowing their little hearts were filled with good intentions, Sarah controlled the urge to check in on them.

She curled up on the couch with the blanket Katie had brought for her the night before to warm her and fell into a sleepy nap, while Daniel "took care of some things" in another part of the house.

Several hours later, Katie emerged with Jonathan following her, helping to drag and push a large box. They had filled an empty box she found in the garage with "secret" gifts to put under the tree—if and when they had one. Carefully "hiding" the box of goodies in the front hall coat closet, she decreed that it should stay there "until the right time" and requested that nobody peek under the blanket she had spread over the treasures.

Daniel had been in the attic and outside in a storage shed he built to hold the kids' bikes and some yard tools. He came into the living room just after Katie and Jonathan managed to get their Christmas goodies into the closet. Seeing their dad with his arms full of boxes and strands of Christmas lights dangling from his neck and hanging off both his arms, the kids let out a shriek that would have awakened the neighbors, had they been deaf!

"Daddy, Daddy, Daddy!" they squealed. "Yaaaaay . . . Yaaaay . . . can we help?" They all pitched in and strung the lights around the windows, hung decorations, and put up their artificial Christmas tree.

Sarah felt so good that she said if the kids wanted to, maybe the next day they could do some Christmas cookie baking—even as she said it she was hoping they had enough ingredients on hand.

"It would be wonderful if we could say thank you to all the wonderful people who gave so much to our family," she added. "I have an idea of how we can make little gift bags by coloring and decorating paper lunch bags. We'll fill each one with our family Christmas baked goods and tie a big bow on each one. How does that sound?"

Jonathan and Katie were so excited about the prospect of making gifts, they wanted to start right in on decorating the bags, which they did.

For the next two days, the entire family baked special Christmas cookies and decorated gift bags. Never had all four of them enjoyed such closeness and quality time together. They had good talks about many things that deepened the bond between them. Soon they had the most amazing lineup of colorful Christmas bags filled with goodies—each with a special note of thanks and giving off the most divine fragrances of cinnamon, peppermint, and vanilla.

Since it was Christmas Eve, Daniel said he would bring the gifts to the church, where Father Cassidy would make arrangements for delivering them. Sarah was advised not to risk exposing her still sensitive immune system to crowds, so the Gomez family planned their own private Christmas service at home.

When Daniel arrived back home, the family read the Christmas story from the Bible and recounted the supernatural miracle of Sarah's healing and being home for Christmas. Katie pulled out the mystery box from the closet, which was full of the things she and Jonathan had found around the house and wrapped with pictures they had colored so they would have some gifts to put under their tree.

Sarah and Daniel were astonished that not a single word was mentioned about Santa Claus coming that night when the kids were tucked into bed.

Several hours later, as they were brushing their teeth and getting ready for bed themselves, they thought they heard bells ringing outside.

"Did you hear that?" Sarah asked. They listened very intently and all was quiet.

"We must be hearing things," Daniel said, then added, "but I sure thought—"

He hadn't even finished his sentence when they distinctly heard what sounded like loud sleigh bells, and then the doorbell rang. They both ran to the front room and peeked out the window. Not seeing anything, but just to be sure, Daniel opened the front door to behold a huge plastic bag with red and green and stars all over it.

"What in the world is this?" they both said in harmony. Daniel noticed a tag reading: "From Santa to the Gomez family"—so he carried the bag into the living room. It was completely filled with beautifully wrapped gifts, mostly for the kids, but there were several for Sarah and Daniel, too.

As they put the presents under the tree, tears of joy streamed down both their faces. This would be a Christmas they would never forget; one that through the caring and selfless giving of others had enriched their lives and deepened their bonds. They also knew that even if there had not been any gifts at all, the true treasures were found in faith, prayer, and each other. The miracles of this Christmas would last them a lifetime.

*P*rayer can heal and transform a person's life any time of the year, but Delores Baca is convinced that prayers for mercy on the behalf of people in trouble have extra power during the Christmas season—and such prayers might even produce a special Christmas angel that can work a miracle, just as it happened for her.

A mother of three daughters who lives near Anaheim, California, Mrs. Baca had become a faithful member of the church prayer group that had been established by their priest.

"Father Gomez instituted a wonderful home enrichment program," she said. "Those of us who wished could gather in one another's homes in groups and join with like-minded people who felt strength and unity in prayer. I will be forever grateful to God that I was a member of such a group, for just before Christmas in 1994, our prayers miraculously helped to save the life of my oldest daughter, Linda."

One night in December when it was her turn to host and to conduct the prayer circle, Delores had a sudden frightening vision of Linda, who was driving home from college for Christmas vacation.

"Since I knew she would be leaving for home that day from Sacramento, I had been concerned all afternoon about her safety," Delores said. "When the terrible images first appeared in my thoughts, I was fearful that my own anxiety was just creating negative pictures in my mind. But then, I reasoned, I surely did not have to be embarrassed to ask my prayer partners to pray with me for my daughter's safety."

Before she could make the request, however, she received a terrible mental picture of Linda approaching a very dangerous stretch of highway.

"My inner vision seemed to take on a life of its own," Delores said. "It was as if I was watching a motion picture beyond my control."

Then, she remembers, she gasped aloud, hoping with all her mother's love that she was not seeing a true image of what was happening to Linda.

"I saw her car being struck by a large truck at a desolate intersection," she said. "I felt as though I would faint when I saw in my mind's eye Linda's car being nearly demolished by the violent impact."

Several of Delores Baca's prayer partners had noticed her anxious behavior, and they asked what was so troubling to her. Delores rose unsteadily to her feet and in a voice trembling with concern, she asked each of the twelve women assembled in her living room that evening to pray for Linda's safety.

"It was at the very moment that I declared my heart-felt plea for their prayers that the miracle occurred," Delores said. "As I spoke the last word of my request for prayers for Linda, an overpowering spiritual presence seemed to enter the room and envelop everyone in it. I beheld a beautiful angelic figure clothed in gold-and-white light walk through the very midst of our prayer group and command, pray!

"Later, at least eight of the women said that they had also seen the beautiful angel of light, and everyone in the group had heard and heeded the command to pray for Linda as she traveled on the highway," Delores said. "Each of us bowed our head in prayer, and we con-tinued our supplication for about thirty minutes. At that time, we all heard the angel's voice say, 'It is past.' "

Late that evening when Linda arrived home, she told her parents and sisters of the harrowing experience that she had undergone while on the road. She had been crossing an intersection in a rather desolate area of highway when the brakes of a heavily loaded truck failed and sent it speeding unchecked directly at her car.

"It would have struck me broadside," Linda said, shaking her head in bewildered memory of the near-fatal experience. "I should have been history. But somehow my car gave a sudden lurch and literally propelled me out of the truck's path. It almost felt as if my car were some kind of living thing that had the power to jump out of the truck's path. Or, even weirder, it kind of felt as though something just lifted my car out of harm's way."

When Delores informed Linda of her vision of the accident, the combined power of the prayer group, and the manifestation of the angel of light, she was extremely moved.

"That would have been at exactly the time that I was approaching the intersection," Linda verified. She sat for a few moments in complete silence, then she crossed herself and said that she must set out at once for church to light candles and to offer prayers of thanksgiving.

Delores said that the entire family accompanied Linda to the church that night.

"We all felt the need to kneel and give thanks for Linda's deliverance," she said. "I cannot explain why the beautiful heavenly being of light chose to answer my pleas and lend its mighty energy and divine power to our prayer group that night. I have not always lived an exemplary life, but I shall be everlastingly grateful that the angel of the Lord had mercy and overlooked my trespasses and saved my daughter's life. Such a miracle was the most wonderful Christmas gift I have ever received."

On Christmas morning, 1957, Mrs. Oleta A. Martin was straightening up the house for her children, who had arrived the night before with their families for a holiday dinner with all the trimmings. Then, suddenly, a pain near her heart made breathing so difficult that she could not even form words to call for help.

Her youngest daughter saw her agony and ran upstairs to awaken the rest of the late-sleeping family.

Oleta's husband moved her to a sofa, and the entire family stood by, helplessly watching the woman in her excruciating pain. Someone went to call for an ambulance.

Oleta Martin's eyes closed and she said later ("My Proof of Survival," *Fate* magazine, June 1969) that she thought she was dying. She seemed to be floating away, and she lost all sensation of pain and all awareness of her surroundings.

When she stopped floating, she found herself at the edge of a wide chasm. It was so dark beneath her that she could not see the bottom. At first she experienced great fear, then calm, when a bright "spiritual" light appeared on the other side of the abyss.

She could make out the general form of a manlike being in the midst of the light, but the illumination was so brilliant that she couldn't distinguish any part of him from his shoulders up.

To the entity's left stood a dozen or so other beings in long, white garments. They seemed to be telling her not to be afraid, that she could cross the chasm without danger and that they would be waiting for her on the other side.

Oleta Martin remembered that she was eager to join them, but the awareness was heavy upon her that once she crossed that wide chasm she would never return. She thought of how greatly her youngest daughter still needed her and how much she would miss being a part of the rest of the family's individual lives.

The pressure on her chest returned. She gasped for breath and again became aware of the room around her. She opened her eyes wider to see her family's tears of worry and grief change to shouts of joyful surprise when they saw that she had smiled weakly.

Her assembled family members cried out "Mother!" in unison and moved toward her as one, but the paramedics who had arrived with the ambulance held them back with a warning that she had just had a very close call and must not become excited.

After a checkup at the clinic, Mrs. Martin gradually improved her heart condition with rest, medication, and a change of diet. Because of her Christmas miracle, she was given another chance to prepare for a more timely opportunity to cross the great chasm to the other side where the heavenly beings await her.

*M*ike McGuire had a wife and six kids to support. He worked as a welder on a city maintenance crew in a large New England city from 6:30 A.M. to 3:30 A.M. and had a part-time job as an attendant at a self-serve gas station from 7:00 P.M. until midnight three nights a week. With six children, ages ranging from two to seventeen, eagerly counting the nights until Christmas Eve, Mike was trying to get as much overtime pay as he could so he could really pile up the presents under the tree. Everyone who knew Mike knew how crazy he was about his kids.

By 3:15 that afternoon, two days before Christmas Eve in 1991, the power-shovel crew had laid the last pipe in place for the day. At 3:30 sharp, the rest of the crew knocked off work for the day, but McGuire did not have to report for work at the gas station that night, so he decided to pick up some overtime by finishing the welding on the seam between the last two pipes in the trench.

"Mike, I'll buy you a beer, man," his best friend Jimmy Wissler told him. "C'mon, it's cold out here. Let's warm up before we head for home."

McGuire grinned at his buddy, Jimmy the bachelor, who never understood about paying dentist bills for braces and buying shoes for six pairs of feet that never seemed to stop outgrowing the new ones you'd bought just three months before.

"I'll take a raincheck, Jimmy," McGuire told him. "This is my last chance for overtime before Christmas. Got to take it, man."

Jimmy shrugged, waved a goodnight, and walked away to leave McGuire to crawl back down into the fourteen-foot trench that housed the new water pipes for a soon-to-open housing district.

"I had just finished my work on the inside seam and was about to begin on the outside of the joint when tons of earth, clay, and stones caved in around and upon me," Mike McGuire said. "I had absolutely no warning of any kind. The damn trench had caved in on me silently and suddenly, as if it had just been waiting to trap me."

McGuire was knocked down in a kneeling position against the big pipe. His nose was crunched up against the plate of his welding mask. For a few moments, he was conscious of searing pain as his right shoulder was pressed against the hot weld he had been making on the pipes. In agony, he tried desperately to squirm away from the burning pipe, but the press of the cave-in held his shoulder fast against the red-hot weld.

"The fact that I had been wearing my welding mask saved my life," he said. "Without the pocket that the mask made around my face, the loose dirt would have covered my nose and mouth—and I would soon have suffocated."

He lay very still, taking stock of his situation.

"I had been covered by a cave-in in a trench in a new housing district where there would probably be little if any traffic. That was definitely a negative," he reasoned in his interior monologue.

"The rest of the crew had gone home—and I was all alone. That was a really big negative.

"My nose hurt like blazes and it was bleeding. I figured it was broken. That was a pretty big negative.

"I had no idea how long I could continue to breathe in this air pocket before I would suffocate. Another negative. A really big negative. There really didn't seem to be any positives at all."

McGuire tried hard not to slip into complete despair, but it seemed that his only chance was that some passersby might have occasion to walk by the trench and notice the cave-in.

But why would they think there was anyone buried in the cave-in? How would they be able to see him?

The terrible realization that there would be no one to come to his rescue began to slice away at the thin mental barrier that had saved him from immediate panic.

"Sure, I knew that my wife Megan would start missing me if I was late for supper," he reasoned, "but it would be hours before she would want to trouble my boss or Jimmy and ask about me. And by then, I could be long suffocated."

Then McGuire realized that his right hand was sticking up through the dirt!

"I could feel the cold air against my open palm and fingers," he said. "Somehow, when the force of the cave-in had struck me, my right shoulder had been pressed against the hot weld and my right arm had been straightened back and above my body, thus allowing my hand to remain above the surface, free to wave like a lonely five-fingered flag. That hand could be my salvation. And the fact that my hand was above the dirt also told me that the cave-in had been very uneven and there wasn't fourteen feet of earth, clay, and stones above me, but only a few feet."

But those were feet of earth heavy enough to prevent McGuire from rising from his kneeling position against the big pipe.

"I had hoped to be able to push the dirt away from my shoulders and stand up," he said. "But there were hundreds of pounds of clay and stones on top of me."

The muscles in his legs were cramping from being forced into a kneeling position, and it was becoming difficult to breathe.

He had been fortunate in having been forced up against the large pipe, thereby creating air pockets near him. But the blood from his broken nose kept dripping into his throat, and he feared that he would soon choke and strangle on it. He was sickened by the thought of drowning in his own blood.

McGuire thought of his wife and his children, and he was startled by the vividness of their images on his mental viewing screen. It truly seemed as if each member of his family had suddenly entered the terrible trench to be with him in his anguish.

"The more I thought about my family, the more I wanted to be with them," he said. "And when I remembered that it was soon Christmas Eve, I was nearly overcome with despair. What a miserable, hell-ish Christmas present I would be giving my family if I didn't somehow get out of this damn trench. But how was I going to accomplish that miracle?"

Each breath that Mike McGuire took was beginning to feel like molten lava being forced into his nostrils.

Then, the next thing he knew, he seemed to be floating above the trench.

"I figure now that I must have passed out and left my body, but then I thought for certain that I had died," he said. "I could see my hand kind of drooping down over a bit of my wrist sticking out above the dirt. I didn't really seem to care about what had happened to me. That's the way it goes. Tough. Too bad.

"But then I thought of my family—and just like that, I was there in the kitchen of my home and feeling terrible sadness and longing," McGuire continued. "My wife Megan was there peeling potatoes for the evening meal. Katie, my oldest girl, was helping her. I went through the rest of the house and saw each one of the kids. Some were watching television. Others were doing their homework. I wanted to hug them one last time. I wanted them to see me. That's when I felt really sad. I didn't want to leave Megan and the kids. I wanted to live."

McGuire remembered that he seemed to float into the kitchen and that he got right up next to his wife's shoulder. "I tried to scream in her ear that I needed help, but she couldn't hear me. Next, I reached out to touch her—and whether or not it was coincidence, she jerked around with a surprised look on her face. I tried screaming again, 'Call the boss. Call Jimmy Wissler!' But I just couldn't get through to her."

Then McGuire found himself back in his pain-cramped body, gasping for the last breaths of air in the pocket around the pipe. "I knew then that I wasn't dead—yet," he said. "But there was some inner voice that told me that I really had been floating out of my physical body and having a last look at my wife and kids. And that same inner voice was telling me that I could do it again."

But this time, McGuire thought he would try to travel to Jimmy and somehow get his best friend to see or hear him. "Old Bachelor Jimmy would be having a cool one at our buddy Squint's bar. He would be sitting there without a care in the world. I just prayed that he wouldn't be shooting pool or something with the boys and hooting and hollering."

McGuire recalled that he only had to think of his friend and he was there beside him. "I gave thanks to the Almighty that Jimmy was just sitting quietly all alone at a table in the corner. I could see his wrist-watch because he had slipped out of his heavy coat and rolled up the sleeves on his sweatshirt. It was 4:35. I had probably been trapped in the cave-in for about forty-five minutes! I could be taking my last breath any minute."

Mike McGuire said later that as he seemed to float above his friend, he could actually see certain things that he was thinking. "Jimmy's thoughts were kind of all jumbled up, like in a dream. I suppose it was because he was just sitting there relaxing, daydreaming—and maybe that's how I got through to him. It wasn't like Megan, peeling potatoes, concentrating on her cooking . . . listening to Katie tell about her new boyfriend . . . hearing the roar of laughter, shouting, and arguing from the other kids in the other rooms . . . trying to mute out the blare of television commercials and the latest hits on the DJ radio show. When I concentrated on Jimmy and said, 'Hey, man, it's Mike. I need you, buddy. I'm trapped in a cave-in at the trench,' he set down his beer bottle and his eyes opened wide."

Jimmy frowned, then said Mike's name aloud. He got up from the table, walked to the bar, and stared hard at himself in the mirror behind the pyramids of bottles and glasses.

Squint asked him what was wrong. "You look like you're looking at a ghost, man."

"You believe in ESP? Telepathy, that sort of thing?" Jimmy asked the bartender.

"Sure," Squint laughed. "I'm Irish, ain't I? And speaking of the Irish, where's your buddy, McGuire?"

McGuire remembered that he prayed that Jimmy and Squint wouldn't get into any philosophical discussion.

"Oh, dear God," Mike thought with all his mind and spirit, "Forgive me my sins. Send your angels to watch over Megan and the kids if I don't make it. But please get Jimmy over here fast. Dear lord, I'm fading away."

The next thing Mike McGuire knew, strong hands were pulling at him, and as if from very far away, he could hear a lot of excited voices. Above all the noise and confusion, he could hear Jimmy telling everyone to take it easy with him.

"For quite a while there, I was still confused," McGuire said. "I really didn't know if I was still floating around like some ghost, or if I was really back in my physical body. Right away, I was frightened, because I thought that my mind was just playing tricks on me and that I was really dead. Then a wonderful kind of peace came over me, and when I opened my eyes again, I was in the hospital and Megan and all the kids were crowded around the bed."

Jimmy Wissler was there, too. And later, when Mike felt better, his friend told him how he had at first heard Mike's voice inside his head, crying out for help.

"I had really been nervous about leaving you there alone, man, you worrying about getting your overtime pay in time for Christmas," Jimmy said. "And I guess you were really on my mind. For a minute there, I thought it was just my worries playing tricks with me, but then, Mike, I swear I saw a vision of you all covered up with clay and stones in that trench. And then I heard your voice again, asking me to come quick and help you. I'm glad I believe in these kinds of things, because the paramedics and the doctors said that we didn't have a whole lot of time to spare. You were sucking the last drops of air from the pocket around you, buddy."

Megan was extremely upset when she learned of the risk in which her husband had placed himself in order to gain some extra money for Christmas presents.

"You are more important to us than any gift you might put under the Christmas tree could ever be," she told him. "You should know by now that Christmas is about far more than presents. The love you give us is what matters to us."

Mike felt the tears come when all the kids chimed in and thanked God for the Christmas miracle that had saved their father's life.

"And Jimmy was our Christmas angel," Katie McGuire said, giving her father's friend a warm hug. "We'll never forget what you did for us tonight, Jimmy."

Jimmy the Bachelor had to excuse himself to get a tissue to remove the "something" that had gotten into his eye and made it tear up all of a sudden.

*D*uring the mid- to-late 1960s, through an innovative Graduate School Professor Exchange Program offered by the Lutheran School of Theology at Chicago, Sherry Hansen Steiger considered herself fortunate to have taken courses from Dr. Elisabeth Kubler-Ross, who was soon to become internationally famous for her pioneering work with dying patients. While attending Dr. Ross's courses, such as "Church History in Psychoanalytic Perspective" and "On Death and Dying," Sherry quite frequently brought her infant son, Erik, bedding him down on a blanket in the back of the classroom.

Sherry was immediately taken with her professor's research into the death process, for even during her undergraduate work in nursing, she had had the first-hand opportunity to observe that dying patients often experienced an encounter with the supernatural. On those occasions when one of her patients had miraculously "come back to life" after a near-death experience, Sherry had witnessed that their lives seemed transformed by what they had seen on the other side.

During one of her lectures, Dr. Kubler-Ross remarked that in her experiences working with dying children, it seemed as if they always knew in advance when they were going to die. Regretfully, she commented, not many doctors or nurses—or even parents—would pay adequate attention to the messages that dying children gave of their awareness of what was imminent in their lives. Understandably, Dr. Kubler-Ross stated, most of the time everyone involved with the child preferred to think only positively and to focus on the prospect that the child would survive the crisis and live.

Perhaps because in Dr. Kubler-Ross Sherry had an extraordinary teacher—who in later years would become a dear personal friend—she was more attuned to the messages that her son Erik would one day attempt to convey regarding his approaching death. Of course, accepting the reality of existence without her dear son would be an entirely different matter.

The 60s were a time of great personal and social upheaval. A time when religious, moral, political, and individual values and belief systems were torn apart, questioned, and often re-evaluated beyond recognition.

We were a nation in crisis and Chicago was at the very heart of the turmoil. The Lutheran School of Theology was a new multimillion-dollar building, located on the south side of Chicago, and on a street declared the "neutral" zone between two very active rival and warring gangs: the Blackstone Rangers and the Devil's Disciples. LSTC was itself in crisis with unrest and dissention from some of the students regarding more relevant curriculum in dealing with the moral issues of the day, of anti-war protesting and security issues in living in such a dangerous area. LSTC was quite literally under attack, and was considered an ostentatious threat and an affront to most of the surrounding ghetto community.

A myriad of experts, special-task forces, various committees, and cadres who had been called in for problem solving and negotiating failed at their attempts to address the various situations threatening the school, staff, and students. Sherry found she could no longer hold back. Presenting what she considered to be very simple, obvious, and apparently overlooked solutions with her own thoughts and ideas to Seminary officials, Sherry was soon asked to repeat her "plan" to the Graduate School's Board of Directors. Following several additional meetings where she was queried regarding the specifics of how she envisioned such a plan implemented, Sherry was offered a position on the staff of LSTC, where she was asked to carry out the job description she had inadvertently created!

Dealing with such intense social issues and "helping others"—whether it is through the ministry or any other service-oriented job—does not provide in exchange immunity to one's own problems, but in fact can often serve to mask them. Perhaps especially during the tumultuous times in the '60s and '70s, many couples who were so immersed in helping others through the times of crisis would find little time to realize they were in crisis themselves, and Sherry and Paul were one such couple. It is never a planned or desired thing when families drift apart, but after considerable effort at attempting to resurrect a failing marriage, Sherry and Paul agreed to divorce in the mid-'70s.

In 1973, the family had embarked on a new venture to the rocky-mountain-high state of Colorado. An idea they had been working on for a creative "seed ministry" together had been planted and risks were taken to tend to the newly sprouted seeds, but the vision wasn't yet rooted in deep enough to weather the many obstacles and unforeseen storms.

Following a period of separation, it was decided that Sherry and daughter Melissa would remain in Colorado while Paul would eventually accept a call from a small rural church in Ohio. It was Paul's conviction that Erik should be with his father and Melissa with her mother, so after much consideration and debate it was decided how to go about the daunting task of telling the children. They took great care in making certain that both Erik and Melissa knew how much they were both loved by both parents and that this was in no way a result of anything they did, as children so often feel in such situations.

Sherry would decide to relocate to Virginia Beach, Virginia, as it would only be a day's drive back and forth to Ohio, enabling easier and more frequent trips for the kids to stay in close contact. So, Melissa and Mom moved to Virginia Beach, and Erik went with Dad to Ohio.

After only several days, Erik was "acting out" and Paul was calling daily to report problems that Erik was having adjusting to the situation and to seek counsel as to how best to deal with it. Paul thought it best not to let Erik talk to his mom until a little more time passed, in hopes that things might balance out and Erik get more accustomed to a new regiment. But nothing seemed to help and the situation escalated with Erik's distress growing. It was later that month that Erik's mounting trauma would result in hospitalization, where tests would reveal a minor heart problem and stress and anxiety, most likely caused by the separation.

Because of her son's intensely traumatic response to the situation, Sherry cancelled the divorce proceedings on December 1. Although her decision to live separate from her husband remained firm, she agreed to travel to Ohio during the Christmas season to reunite the family for the holiday. Paul had come to realize, albeit painfully, that Erik wanted to be with Sherry, but the burden of losing his entire family during the pressures of Christmas, the busiest season of the year for pastors, was more than he felt capable of managing at that time. Sherry and Melissa left their home in Virginia Beach and drove to the parish in Ohio, where they even became somewhat involved in the church functions, as Sherry loved the warm, friendly country spirit of the parishioners.

Sherry later remembered that it was at Erik's school Christmas pageant that she received an almost unbearable glimpse into the future. As she proudly watched her son singing Christmas carols on the auditorium stage, Erik's red hair appeared to have an extra-shiny gleam and the stage lights seemed to capture every freckle on the face that she loved so much. His whole manner seemed to exude an extra-joyful spirit, and he appeared to be ablaze with the excitement of Christmas and the knowledge that his mommy and little sister were back in his life again.

Although Sherry sat with Melissa on her lap in seats that were midway toward the back of the large auditorium, she sensed a strange feeling of oneness with her son. While the class was singing "The Little Drummer Boy," Erik's favorite Christmas carol, a terrible uneasiness crept up to seize her solar plexus and her throat. The next selection of the children's chorus, "Away in a Manger," forced her eyes to well up with tears.

As the children sang the words "no crib for his bed," a surreal scene was frozen in a stopgap of time in Sherry's mind. She will remember it always as if a camera lens had focused in for a close-up, and then captured the image in a freeze-frame. And then a voice from out of nowhere said ever so clearly to Sherry: "This is the last Christmas you'll see your son."

"It was as though I had been struck a cruel and vicious blow to my stomach," Sherry said. "The psychic pain was so overwhelming that it was little Melissa who jolted me back into reality."

Melissa was actually shaking her and asking if she was all right. "Why are you crying, Mommy?" she wanted to know. "Isn't this a happy time?"

Suddenly aware that she was weeping, Sherry wiped her tears away and tried to regain her composure. "Yes, sweetie, yes, it is a time to be happy," she told Melissa. "I guess Mommy was just crying tears of joy."

Although the terrifying freeze-frame image of Erik and the awful message still pierced her heart, Sherry saw that Melissa was comforted by her explanation.

The remainder of that evening proceeded as normal—except for the memory of the troubling vision that haunted Sherry and forced her again and again to attempt to understand its exact meaning.

Then came the special midweek children's Christmas service at the church where Paul served as pastor.

"The church was packed," Sherry recalled. "It was customary for all the children of the congregation to gather at the steps near the altar, while the pastor gave a sermon just for them."

Children from under two years to ten were all excitedly sitting on the steps, listening to the pastor deliver a Christmas message structured to teach them the true meaning of the holiday. It was baby Jesus' birthday, and the pastor pointed to the manger scene under the decorated tree.

After the brief sermon, Pastor Paul posed a question for the gathered children. "What gift would you give the baby Jesus?" he asked, going on to create a colorful scenario. "Since it is baby Jesus' birthday, let's pretend that you are invited to his birthday party and you can take him any gift you wanted to. What gift would you bring him?"

Pausing to emphasize the seriousness of the query, the pastor said, "I want you to really think about it. Then, when you are ready, I want you to tell everyone here tonight what your gift would be."

It took only a few seconds for the children, one by one, to seem satisfied that they had selected the perfect gift for the baby Jesus. A little boy offered his toy fire engine. A girl was willing to give up her favorite doll. Another little girl said that she would give baby Jesus her very favorite cuddly teddy bear, the one that went with her everywhere.

Sherry could almost hear the wheels turning in Melissa's head as she thought about her own birthday, which was just days away. Melissa was nearly born on Christmas Day herself. She would be four years old on the day after Christmas, December 26. "I'd give baby Jesus my love," she said emphatically.

"I was very touched by Melissa's response," Sherry said, "and I smiled back at those members of the congregation who turned to me with warm smiles, silently bespeaking, 'Oh, how sweet, how precious.' "

Then came Erik's turn. "He was not a shy boy," Sherry said, recalling the scene of that long-ago Christmas service. "Erik had something of an impish element to him. He liked to tease and play. In a situation such as this, he might be embarrassed and say something cute or silly to make people laugh."

But Sherry noticed how serious Erik was as his father, Pastor Paul, prompted him, "Erik, what would you give baby Jesus?"

Looking directly at the image of the baby Jesus in the manger, Erik turned and spoke boldly and with conviction: "I'd give him my soul!"

"The tears in my eyes welled instantly to overflowing," Sherry said. "I choked back a gasp as I could not help being reminded of the 'freeze-frame' incident days earlier and the horrible message that had come with it that this would be the last Christmas that I would see my son. No! rang through my head so loudly that I was certain others could hear it."

Sherry stated that she has no memory of what took place between Erik's declaring the gift of his very soul to baby Jesus and the final blessing of the pastor at the end of the service.

"I stood there, shaking hands with members of the congregation in an altered state of consciousness," she said. "I was stuck somewhere among my thoughts and the terrible confusion that I felt."

So many strange little things occurred in the days that followed. And some of them were harbingers of the awful events that lay ahead.

"Paul took the kids in his van to pick up a baby-sitter and the driver's door kept flying open as he drove down the snow-and-ice packed country road," Sherry said. "When they returned, Erik came bolting in the front door, laughing and declaring how much fun it had been to be in the van when it spun around and around on the ice. To his child's mind, to spin on the ice wasn't dangerous; it was like an amusement park ride. As he described the door opening and the van spinning in circles on the ice-packed road, I felt my face go white."

On the next two mornings, totally out of character, Erik arose first and knelt at his mommy's bedside. "Erik was one who didn't like to get up in the morning," Sherry said, "so I was shocked to see him kneeling there and staring at me. When I asked him if something was wrong, he answered, 'Nothing's wrong, Mommy. I just love you so very much, that's all.'"

Sherry awakened to see Erik kneeling at her bedside for the third morning in a row. Once again, he assured her that nothing was wrong. She slipped back asleep, but a little while later, Erik once again came back into the room and told her that he had a present for her.

"He took me by the hand and led me into the playroom where he had assembled a puzzle that pictured a single white horse grazing in a beautiful green meadow," Sherry said. "I hugged him and gave him a kiss, and he solemnly informed me that the puzzle could not be disassembled and put away. It was a present for me."

With so many other things on her mind, Sherry agreed to Erik's request. It seemed very strange to her that he had taken such great pride in the accomplishment of having pieced this particular puzzle together.

From the time he was very small, he had always been the greatest of puzzle solvers and assemblers. This was a very simple fifty-or-so piece puzzle, the kind that he had put together effortlessly when he was three or four years old.

But she had more pressing matters to consider. It was now time to get ready for church on Christmas Sunday—and the weather was formidable. It was sleeting, snowing, and blowing, and extremely cold.

Paul had left for church quite some time earlier, and there had already been three or four phone calls from concerned parishioners warning Sherry not to venture out on such bad roads. Pastor Hansen's house was out in the country, and it was about a twenty-minute drive to church.

"Don't you feel that you have to come out because it's Christmas Sunday or because of Pastor Paul or any other reason," one earnest lady had told her over the telephone. "The roads are terrible and dangerous. There are warnings for folks to stay inside. All of the other churches in the entire surrounding area are closed. Pastor insists that he will hold services for whoever wants to make it out since he's already there. But we don't want anything to happen to you and the kids. Just stay in and be safe."

Sherry felt pleased with the sincere expressions of concern, but since she and the kids were all ready, she decided that they might as well go—carefully—to church.

"Not until I was in the garage trying to open the door to my Fiat convertible did I realize how really bad the weather was," Sherry said. "My car had been in the shop getting a new top, and this was the first time I had gone out to drive since I brought it back from the garage. The doors wouldn't open. They were frozen shut."

Sherry tried a hammer and boiling water. Nothing would budge those doors.

After about twenty minutes of failed efforts, Erik said, "Good, Mom. Let's just go in and build a fire and you can read us a story."

That sounded like the perfect plan to Sherry. But Melissa wasn't satisfied with it. "No, let's go to church," she yelled. "We can take the jeep."

Sherry walked over to the jeep that had been loaned to Pastor Paul by some parishioners. She said that she had never driven such a vehicle, and she would have no idea where the keys were kept.

"Daddy always leaves the keys in the ignition," Melissa said.

Sure enough, they were there.

Sherry turned the keys in the ignition but got no response from the engine. After a second and third attempt, she concluded that trying to start the jeep was a waste of time. "Okay, kids," she said, "let's go into the house and build a fire."

For some reason, such a pronouncement made Melissa start to cry and insist that she wanted to go to church.

"I suspected that the reason behind Melissa's youthful dedication to church was a normal desire to play with other children her own age in the nursery," Sherry said, "but I gave the jeep one more try. This time it started."

As she looked over at her two children, half-crouched and half-standing on the passenger side's bucket seat, for the first time the flimsy structure of the loaned jeep became apparent to her. It was really more or less a customized vehicle that had been hand-built from an army surplus kit. And it didn't even have seatbelts.

"After all the attempts to open my car door and to start the homemade jeep, it occurred to me that we would end up being late for services anyway," Sherry said, "but I started out very carefully on the hazardous country road. The maximum speed that I would dare drive was about fifteen to twenty-five miles an hour. But I thought that even if we arrived for only the last fifteen minutes of church, at least we would have been there."

When they were about halfway to the church, the passenger door of the jeep flew open. Since they were traveling at a slow speed, Sherry came to a near stop and Erik pulled the door shut. But it came open again and again.

"That does it," Sherry exclaimed. "We are definitely not taking this back home."

When they finally arrived at the church, they went to one of the back pews and quietly sat down. The service had been late to start, granting a little extra time for those who chose to brave the bad weather.

"Erik and Melissa seemed amazingly loving with one another during the service," Sherry remembered. "Once I turned just in time to watch Erik remove his cherished Native American Star necklace and silently place it around his sister's neck. He was never without that necklace. It was his most treasured possession. And now, with a kiss on her cheek, he had bestowed it upon Melissa. In turn, Melissa removed her beloved linked chain with the 'fish that wiggled' and placed it around Erik's neck, positioning the little fish just so."

Sherry felt a strange reaction to the sweet scene of sibling affection. "My kids had performed what seemed to be a sacred act, vowing to one another their love," she said, "yet I felt a rush of panic similar to the ones that I had felt at the school auditorium, at the children's Sunday school Christmas service, upon hearing about the van spinning on the ice, and upon viewing Erik's gift of the white horse puzzle."

She had always been one to pay heed to signs seemingly sent by a higher power to communicate assistance and to ward off danger. Many times her premonitions had saved the very lives of her family and friends. She suddenly felt guilty, wondering if she had acted irresponsibly by not staying home in the safety of a warm farmhouse.

Sherry was mouthing the final liturgy of the service when she received a strong mental and physical picture of the jeep's door flying open on its own. A firm conviction took hold of her. She would not drive the jeep home.

During the customary shaking of hands with the congregants at the door, Sherry made her appeal to Paul. She told him that she had to take the jeep since the doors on her car were frozen shut. The jeep had no seatbelts, and its passenger door had kept flying open all the way to church, endangering the lives of the kids, who had to sit huddled next to her to keep from falling out.

"I am not taking it home," Sherry said firmly. "I have a bad feeling about it. I'll leave it in the church parking lot and someone can pick it up later."

Paul seemed to ignore her, concentrating on greeting the parishioners. When he did answer her, he completely astonished her by stating that she would have to get permission from the family who owned the jeep to leave it in the church parking lot.

As if trapped in some incredible drama of the absurd, Sherry spent the next ten minutes pleading with the individual members of the "jeep family" for permission to leave their makeshift vehicle in the parking lot so she and her children could ride home with Pastor Paul. Incredibly, they were all unwilling to grant her this favor. They had plans so none of them could drive their vehicle to their home, and they adamantly refused to allow it to sit unattended in the parking lot.

Then Paul told her that he could not take her and the kids with him in the van, because he had promised to take some of the elderly home, and then he had to return to the church for those who wished to sing Christmas carols.

With a growing sense of mounting doom, Sherry could no longer hold back tears of frustration. Speaking as firmly as her ebbing strength permitted, she said to Paul, "I feel so strongly about this. I insist that the children go with you. If I have to take the jeep without any seatbelts and a door that won't stay shut, fine. But Melissa and Erik are not going to be in it with me."

At last, with obvious irritation, Pastor Paul agreed. He locked the church doors as Sherry made certain that Erik and Melissa were in the van.

As Paul hurriedly raced toward the van, Sherry rolled down the window of the jeep and asked that they stay close together because the weather was so bad. "I'll follow you," she said. "Keep watching for me out your back window."

He nodded agreement and climbed into the van, slamming the door behind him.

Sherry saw that the weather had become even worse. Visibility seemed zero as it continued to snow.

The van pulled to the edge of the parking lot, then suddenly and abruptly came to a halt. Shocked, Sherry saw Erik getting out. Then he was crying and running toward her.

"Erik!" she screamed, rolling down the window once again. "Get back in the van. What on earth are you doing?"

As she watched in disbelief, she saw the van pull out of the parking lot and turn right, leaving Erik behind with her. "No, no, no!" she screamed again and again.

When Erik crawled into the jeep, he was still crying. "What happened, honey?" Sherry asked. "Don't you know that you were supposed to ride with Dad?"

Erik shook his head. "I want to be with you, Mom. I want to be with you."

It was now more than apparent that Paul was not returning with the van to pick up Erik. Sherry got out to check the doors of the church, hoping to find one unlocked. If need be, she and Erik would stay there until Paul returned for the caroling. But no doors had been left open and there was no one in sight.

As Sherry surveyed the grim situation, she came to the inevitable realization that she had no choice other than to embark in the makeshift jeep with Erik.

"Sweetie," she told him, "sit as close to Mommy as possible. Hold on to the back of my seat or to me, just in case the door opens up again. And push down on the lock. Maybe that will help keep the door closed."

The road was slicker than ever and the visibility was almost zero. Sherry could drive only about ten to fifteen miles per hour.

The silence of her concentration on her driving was suddenly broken by what seemed to be a strong mental message coming from Erik: "It's okay, Mom. I love you." She wasn't sure if he didn't actually say it out loud.

At that very instant the jeep hit a bump and began to skid. First they slid to one side of the road, then back to the other. Then something seemed to catch at the right side of the jeep—and it flipped over in the snow.

"I was unable to open the door on the driver's side, so I rolled down the window and climbed out," Sherry said. "I called out Erik's name as I brushed the snow from my long skirt and sweater. Because we had been going so slow, it never dawned on me that he could be injured."

When she received no response from her son, she looked around and saw only the spinning wheels of the jeep, the snow, and the empty fields.

As she walked around to the other side of the vehicle, Sherry half-expected her pixie son to be playing a trick on her. Maybe he was hiding, and he was about to jump out and say, "Boo!"

But still there was no Erik. "I called out his name several times, but heard no answer," Sherry said. "By now I was becoming worried that something must be very wrong."

Then she saw Erik's little feet trapped under the mass of steel. "No!" she cried in a mother's deepest anguish.

Desperately she tried to lift the jeep while trying at the same time to call to her son. "Erik, can you hear me?" she screamed as she tried to move the jeep. Erik made no reply.

Again and again she attempted to lift the jeep off her beloved only son. For years she had read stories in which people under duress had accomplished such a miraculous feat, regardless of how impossible it may have seemed. For even more years, Sherry had worked at her faith. The words of Jesus raced through her mind and mouth: "If you just believe, you shall be healed . . . Nothing is impossible unto you if you so believe!"

She directed every exertion of life energy from every cell of her body and mind into each attempt to lift the jeep and free Erik. She knew that her faith was strong and she did believe.

But no matter how much she strained and pushed and tried, she could budge the jeep by only a few inches. She needed somehow to roll the vehicle over and off her son in order to pull him out. She tried desperately again and again. But she could not do it.

At last a truck that was passing by stopped to assist her. Inside the cab were three stocky men, one of whom was a member of Pastor Paul's church and an off-duty ambulance driver. The men had a CB unit in the truck, so they radioed for an ambulance, then proceeded to set about righting the jeep, shouting at Sherry to pull her son out from under the vehicle as they held it off his body.

In horror Sherry looked at Erik, who appeared not to be breathing. Her nurse's training told her that he should not be moved. "Just roll the jeep off him," she shouted at the men. "He shouldn't be moved until medical help arrives."

Although she shouted the same demand over and over, each time the men retorted, "Just do it! Pull him out, for God's sake!"

Mired once again in a feeling of helplessness, Sherry did as they ordered and pulled Erik out from under the jeep. As soon as he was free, she knelt beside him and placed her coat around his body. She cradled his head in her lap. When she saw the bubbles coming out of his nose, she knew his lungs were damaged.

Completely immersed in grief and despair, Sherry hardly noticed that the ambulance had finally arrived—forty-five minutes after it had been called. The drivers had gotten lost.

Once the paramedics were on the scene, though, they sprang into action. Sherry was dimly aware of shouts of confusion all around her, and she barely perceived that Paul's van was now present. Then she realized that the paramedics had put her on a stretcher and were monitoring her because they had been informed that she had a hole in her heart from a prior condition, and they feared the effects of the stress of the accident could provoke a cardiac incident. Erik was on the stretcher beside her in the ambulance.

Sherry remembered that she kept telling the personnel in the hospital emergency room to leave her alone and to give all their attention to Erik. "I was hooked up to all kinds of equipment, and I prayed aloud, 'Oh, God, please take me and spare my son. Please, please, please! Take me, not Erik!'"

A Catholic priest, a friend of Pastor Paul's, tried to calm her. "You don't know what you're saying," he said. "You can't bargain with God. Only God knows if it is Erik's time and He is calling him home. That is not your decision. It is the Lord's."

Sherry recalled that at that moment she felt very much betrayed by any higher power. "I was suffused only with the desire to sacrifice my life for that of my only son," she said. "I continued to wail in anguish, and I didn't care who heard me."

And then all at once, Sherry was completely silent. There was Erik standing at her bedside. She reached out and took his hand, and her cries of grief gave way to a smile. "Erik," she asked him, "what are you doing up? Are you all right?"

Erik smiled and squeezed her hand. "I'm all right, Mommy. I'm okay. I love you very much, Mommy."

Sherry was distracted by the priest at her side asking her what she was seeing.

"It's Erik," she laughed. "He's all right."

And then the image of her son was gone, and Sherry shrunk back in terror as she saw several doctors and a nurse trailed by Paul burst into the room. She saw the nurse fill another hypodermic needle, and she screamed out, "I don't want another shot! I don't want another—"

Sherry's trailing protest was met with the most dreaded words a mother can ever hear: "I'm sorry. We tried everything. We lost him. He's gone."

The physician had said the awful words as tenderly and as gently as possible, but Sherry would not accept the pronouncement. "No, it can't be. Erik was just here. He told me that he was all right . . . and that he loved me," she told the doctor and the others in the room.

The priest finally broke the silence that had fallen on the hospital room. He squeezed both of Sherry's hands, even more firmly than before. "You are truly blessed to have had Erik appear to you so vividly with such a confirmation," he said. "Erik came to tell you that he is all right. He's with the Lord now, and he is truly at peace. God's will be done."

Since that Christmas Day many years ago, Sherry has often reflected upon the sorrowful episode. "Why, during that last week of his life, did I not take to heart the omens that Erik had been giving me?" she has wondered. "Why could I not perceive the clues that he had been offering, that his time with me, as well as his gift of life, were coming to a close? Was Dr. Kubler-Ross correct about children knowing that they were about to die and that God was calling them home? I can see clearly now that Erik's soul was aware of another calling, one with which he seemed to be at peace."

Sherry has also pondered the meaning of the white horse in the puzzle that Erik was so insistent should have meaning for her. Because she is of Chippewa heritage, as well as French and Swedish, and because she has spent a good deal of time with Native American shamans, Sherry was aware that for many Native American tribes, a vision of a white horse represents Death coming to accompany the spirit to the land of the grandparents. Since his earliest childhood, Erik was enthralled with so many of the mythological aspects of the native tribes, and he was buried with his cherished star necklace, put back on his chest by his sister and his mom. A white horse may also symbolize magic powers, and the enchanted animal may serve as a warrior's ally in transcending the trials and tribulations of Earth.

It is said that the most grievous loss to endure is that of losing a child. "Although the pain never entirely goes away, it brings with it a sort of mystical link to every mother or father who has ever lost a child—under any circumstances—to unfair and untimely death. Since it was Christmas Eve when Erik was buried, how could I not think of the meaning of Christmas of Jesus' birth, and the suffering that not only he would go through, but the suffering and agony of his mother, the Blessed Mother. She too, long before I would lose Erik, would have to endure and accept the death of her beloved son. And so too have many, many mothers and fathers lost their young ones at an all-too-early age, throughout the history of life on earth," Sherry said.

Sherry Hansen Steiger has long been at peace with her son's death, and she has come to realize that she gained a much deeper meaning, design, and purpose to life because of the pain of her loss. She holds dear a poem that Erik gave her just before he died, and she regards it as her son's awareness of the transitory nature of life and his ability to see the act of physical death as being merely the changing of one life form to another. Here is that poem:

> *The caterpillar, brown and furry,*
> *Caterpillar, in a hurry,*
> *Take your walk*
> *To the shady leaf or stalk.*
> *May no toad spy you.*
> *May the little birds pass you by . . .*
> *To live again . . .*
> *a Butterfly.*
>> *Love, Erik*

The biggest lesson that Sherry learned to pass on to others and to apply in her own life is that at any given instant of any given day, our loved ones may be taken from us—or we from them. Knowing this, it seems that the most important thing we could ever do in life would be to live each moment completely with love and fullness, as if it were our very last to be with our loved ones.

If each morning when we awakened we considered the possibility that this might be the last day that we would see our husband or wife, our son or daughter, our mother or father, our sister or brother, how completely that would change how we would respond to them or interact with them. And that, Sherry believes, is the real message of Jesus and the most important message of all faiths and religions: To live each moment in love and caring, selflessly and unconditionally.

What greater Christmas miracle could a mother receive from her son?

On the one hand this Christmas miracle may not seem like a miracle at all, with the death of a very young, vital, and loving boy who will never again see another first snowfall, another tree being trimmed with sparkling, magical lights of another Christmas. Yet on the other hand, in reality not every miracle brings with it what we call a "happy ending."

We include this story not to make you sad, but to remind you that while we rejoice in relating those miracles that accomplish acts of healing, happiness, and wholeness of body, mind, and spirit, in our other stories there is a deeper point we wish to make. Perhaps those miracles that often serve to bring about greater awareness, understanding, insight, and compassion, may not always have warm fuzzy endings. Often we can see the furthest at night. When it is dark and we look into the heavens above us, we can see millions and billions of miles away. On the clearest of days, however, we cannot see further than one mile, if we stand on the ground. So too, it is often through the most painful experiences in life that we are drawn closer to God.

The process of sorting through the pain and breaking free into a greater understanding and spiritual depth necessitates a vulnerability to experience the pain and the grace to know there may be a higher purpose and much more—a divine plan of God's Wisdom at work. It might not be our desired plan—it might not be what we would wish for. It might not have the kind of ending that we ourselves would write—if we could—or plan—if we could. But God is a far better author than we could ever hope to be. It only takes looking at the beauty and rhythm of nature surrounding us on earth, and then viewing the vast, complex infinite beauty, order, and design in the heavens above to realize that The Master of Miracles, our Creator, has done an awesome job in creating the universe and is so much more than a genie in a magic lamp, ready to obey our every wish and command for our human, earthly desires. It might be that we don't know best after all. While we may never completely grasp the greater purpose or divine plan for the way things sometimes unfold and turn out in our individual "life dramas," by having faith and trusting that God does we might draw to ourselves an even greater miracle!

About the Authors

BRAD STEIGER is the author/coauthor of over 100 books with millions of copies in print, covering such diverse subject matter as biographies, true crime, and the paranormal. A former high school/college English and creative writing teacher, Brad's early success as a published author launched him into writing full-time and professionally since 1963. In 1978, Brad's book *Valentino* was made into a motion picture by British film director Ken Russell, starring Rudolf Nureyev. Later that same year, Brad co-scripted the documentary film *Unknown Powers*, winner of the Film Advisory Board's *Award of Excellence* in 1978. Brad is considered one of the leading experts in the field of metaphysics and the paranormal. Among Brad's honors: Metaphysical Writer of the Year, Hypnosis Hall of Fame and Lifetime Achievement Award.

SHERRY HANSEN STEIGER, author/coauthor of twenty-nine books has an extensive background as diverse and varied as a writer, creative director for national advertising agencies, magazine editor, producer, model, and actress to studying the healing arts and theology—traditional and alternative. A former teacher, counselor, and an ordained minister, Sherry co-created and produced the highly acclaimed

Celebrate Life multi-awareness program performed around the country for colleges, businesses, and churches, from the mid-1960s on, and established one of the earliest non-profit schools with new approaches to healing body, mind and spirit—*The Butterfly Center for Transformation.* Among her honors: International Woman of the Year from Cambridge, and Five Hundred Leaders of Influence-Twentieth Century Achievement Award, on permanent display in the U.S. Library of Congress.

Brad and Sherry have been featured in twenty-two episodes of the popular television series, *Could It Be A Miracle.* Together their television appearances and specials include: *The Joan Rivers Show, Entertainment Tonight,* HBO, *Inside Edition, Hard Copy, Hollywood Insider,* USA network, The Arts and Entertainment (A & E) Channel, and The Learning Channel, among others. The Steigers write a monthly angel column for Beliefnet.com and are frequent guests on international radio talk shows.

Visit the Steigers' Web site at *www.bradandsherry.com.*